Lincoln as More Than a Statesman

"The tendency to soften the lineaments of this strange quaint, rugged, and powerful man has been natural, for his heart was as great as his brain; but it does injustice to his most important public aspect, his tough, forcible, hard-hitting side. Too much has been said of this kindness, mildness, and magnanimity. These traits were real, but so were his calculating shrewdness, his firmness, his occasional harshness, and his infrequent but unforgettable bursts of anger. He said "no" with a good-natured air, but he said it often and positively. In dealing with cunning politicians he had a cunning of his own that Stanton called genius. He pardoned sleeping sentries and deserters not merely because he was kindly, but because he had a keen instinct for policy; he was no worshipper of generals, he disliked military despotism, he saw that the North had to depend on masses of volunteers, and he knew that if the regular army officers imposed the death penalty without check, volunteering would stop."

Allan Nevins, Professor of History at Columbia University and twice winner of the Pulitzer Prize, is one of America's most honored Civil War scholars.

S0-AIF-133

ALLAN NEVINS

THE
OF THE

STATESMANSHIP CIVIL WAR

New, Enlarged Edition

COLLIER BOOKS

NEW YORK, N.Y.

This Collier Books edition is published by arrangement with The Macmillan Company

Collier Books is a division of The Crowell-Collier Publishing Company

First Collier Books Edition 1962

Acknowledgments

Chapters 1 and 2 previously appeared in *American Heritage*
Chapters 3, 4 and 6 were the Page-Barbour Lectures given at the University of Virginia in 1951, copyright, 1953 by The Macmillan Company
Chapter 5 previously appeared in *Lincoln*: A *Contemporary Portrait,* Copyright © 1962, by Doubleday & Company, Inc.
Chapter 7 is copyright © 1961, by *Saturday Review*

Introduction

IN WRITING A SERIES OF VOLUMES on the period of sectional conflict, I have been interrupted from time to time by demands for magazine articles or lectures which I could not decline. Some of them, happily, gave me opportunity to ponder a little the lessons of the tumultuous period of national life from the Mexican War to the end of Reconstruction. They enabled me to present an interpretation of certain facets of that manysided era, and to set down a number of conclusions. Most narrative historians are disposed to give their readers all too little interpretive matter; they prefer to let the facts speak for themselves. But the facts have to be given a special arrangement, which is in itself a task of interpretation; and the writer who has spent years upon the details of a period has, or ought to have, a marked advantage in deciphering its significance. He owes it to his public and himself to seek out a hill now and then, climb its tallest rock, and attempt to map the whole forest among whose trees he has been moving.

Inasmuch as some of my fundamental convictions respecting the Civil War are merely implied here, an explicit statement upon them may be useful. I regard the war as a terrible tragedy, a blot upon the record of our democracy, and a subject for sorrowful regret rather than the thoughtless glorification it has sometimes received. Lincoln in his second inaugural took precisely the right attitude toward it. I believe also that from the standpoint of the national government it was a necessary and justifiable war, vindicated by its results. Few men North or South will question the assertion that the interests of the American people and the progress of liberal institutions throughout the world required the preservation of the Union. The abolition of slavery might better have been achieved less abruptly, by gradual well-planned steps; but the freesoil North could not and should not have receded from its position in 1860 that slavery must no longer be allowed to expand into new territories, and that the hour had struck when the country should sit down soberly and think out a scheme, say of gradual compensated emancipation, for terminating the institution. That was all that the Northern majority and the new Administration asked, and it was a completely sound demand.

The consequences of the war, politically, economically, and socially, were vast, but the largest consequence was this: that the North, forced to mobilize and apply its latent energies in a hundred fields to win the conflict, in so doing transformed its whole character. Within five years an unorganized democracy, slack, inchoate, and narrow in vision, was converted into an organized republic, disciplined, efficient, and ready to undertake tasks of continental scope. Although the 600,000 boys who died in the war should have been spared, they did not die in vain. They left behind a country in which Union was perdurable, which by a rough surgical operation had gotten rid of the cancer of slavery, and which by the inexorable demands of war had been forced from adolescence into maturity.

The author is grateful to the Macmillan Company, to Doubleday & Company, to Alfred A. Knopf, Inc., to the *Saturday Review,* and to *American Heritage* for permission to reprint these papers.
The Huntington Library
August 1, 1962

ALLAN NEVINS

Contents

The Statesmanship of the Civil War

Chapter 1

American Crises and American Leadership

BENJAMIN FRANKLIN, as he tells us in his *Autobiography*, once decided upon a plan for systematic self-examination, and continued it some time. "I was surprised to find myself so much fuller of faults than I had imagined," he confesses. Every adult man, surveying his own career, can discern errors of judgment, lapses of conduct, and other missteps which have resulted in sharp penalties if not calamities. Everyone knows how often the adjustability of environment, personal resilience, or a kind fate has justified for him Shakespeare's remark that a divinity shapes our ends, rough-hew them how we may. It would be well if nations were more addicted to self-examination through critical reviews of their pasts. In national careers the role of error, passion, and misconduct may or may not be larger than in the life of the average citizen——that depends on a nation's institutions, which may minimize or maximize the effect of its faults. But it is certainly always great, and to reflective students of history it is often appalling. Some nations, like Russia and Germany, plunge from one crime-tinged

blunder to another, from calamity to calamity. It is by no
means certain that Gibbon was thinking of ancient and
medieval times when he declared that history is a record of
the crimes, follies, and misfortunes of mankind. That
somber remark applies to the modern era just as emphatically.

The career of the American people from 1607 until
today has, on the whole, been the sunniest and most fortunate yet written by a great power. But we dare not say "the
most successful," for criteria of success differ; and a severe
backward look should cure us of any complacency. The
pages have more flaws and stains than many people
suppose.

The three main reasons why the American record has
been exceptionally prosperous both materially and morally
have little connection with any peculiar virtue of the population. Geographical isolation down to recent times,
coupled with the fact that sea power long rested in the
hands of a kindred and friendly nation, gave the United
States security, exempted it from the burden of large military establishments, and fostered its serene optimism. This
relatively unmolested house was also a rich house. Planted
in a virgin continent replete with natural resources, the
American people—while finding in the development of
mine, forest, and prairie a challenge to their energies—
easily learned to elevate their living standards above any
previously made general. And as a third factor, their intan-
gible inheritance was happy in both its negative and its
positive aspects. They inherited only a few vestiges of the
old feudal restraints of Europe, and rapidly shook them off.
But their heritage did include the humanizing literature,
the intellectual liberalism, the principles of political freedom
and tradition of compromise which had developed in
Britain between Magna Charta and the Whig Revolution,
between Chaucer and Milton. This early patrimony successive waves of immigration augmented by importing the
spiritual wealth of other lands.

"America, du has es besser!" In fact, though Goethe's exclamation did not imply this, the United States found its position so much better than that of older nations that its very blessings, like those of a child too rich and talented to know the common lot, might have turned into misfortune. People, like Hercules, gain strength from strangling serpents in their cradles and slaying lions in young manhood. They gain vision from midnight anxieties. However, the republic, as numerous foreign observers were quick to point out, was by no means without certain evils and disabilities. It had some troublesome frontiers, and long-continued difficulties with its aboriginal inhabitants. It had almost unprecedented problems in the assimilation of many varied national stocks, and in stretching one federal government over three million square miles. The labor of subduing its shaggy domain and exploiting its natural resources developed an excessively materialistic temper. Because the people were protected by thousands of miles of salt water on each flank, they tended to become provincial and isolationist, so that the ultimate acceptance of global responsibilities was a painful process. Because they had so much wealth at hand, they tended toward an aggressive individualism, until the palaces of the outrageously rich crowded the slums of the pitiably impoverished.

Most distressing of all, the United States had one problem from which nearly all Europe was free: a terrible race problem. If historians today had that faith in a guiding national Providence which George Bancroft possessed, they might picture it as having decided to add to all its gifts to America one great balancing burden. "See," Providence, or Fate, would say, "this people has every advantage, every resource. They must have one fettering liability. We must throw into America millions of colored folk, to create frictions and tensions, and to compel the people, right down the centuries from John Woolman to Chief Justice Warren and long afterward, to face dark hours of decision, to wage bloody struggles among themselves, and finally to find their salvation in righting heavy wrongs. They shall have one seeming curse among their many benefits." Lincoln, we may remember, credited Providence with just this intention: "If we shall suppose that American Slavery is one of those offences which, in the providence of God, must needs come, but which, having continued through His appointed time, He now wills to remove, and that He gives to both North and South, this terrible war, as the woe due to those by whom the offence came, shall we discern therein any departure from those divine attributes which the believers in a Living God always ascribe to Him?"

But this one burden of slavery and race friction was our ꞏy sore handicap. We had ampler advantages in displayꞏng a sound statesmanship than other lands, and it is therefore the more important to take note of our aberrations. Considering our limited opportunities for blundering, we have made fertile use of them! If our writers had explored the record more candidly and our public had conned it more diligently, we would possess a fuller appreciation of the fact. Why do we lack such an appreciation?

For one reason, our history has been such a shining success story that too often we have thought of every part of it as a success story. For another, like other young, rapidly developing nations, we have had short memories. Our interest in the Future is much keener than in the Past; rapid growth, incessant change, and successive waves of immigration have helped to abbreviate our memories. Then, too, our exuberant nationalism in the early decades of the republic, and our filiopietistic exaltation of our ancestors in that period, made for complacency and an ultra-patriotic belief that we always did right. The tendency around 1820 to overestimate our leadership in the Revolutionary period irritated John Adams, who declared that he had known the leaders well and that they were far from demigods. Thomas Hart Benton, asserting in his *Thirty Years' View* that the inner workings of government from Madison to Polk had been entirely different from the public conception of events, held the same disillusioned opinion of many of the later leaders. Not many countries have over-idealized any chieftain as we have over-idealized Lincoln.

Like other peoples, we have lurched into difficulties and then muddled our way out; but perhaps more than others we have let the ultimate escape obscure the early blundering. That is, we have done what Macaulay said Britons did in looking at Henry V. Reckless King Harry's career was unquestionably a disaster to England and Europe; but Britons forgot all this in recalling the glories of Agincourt. Just so, our victorious sea battles in the War of 1812 have obscured for most Americans the fact that Great Britain then fully asserted her command of the ocean, blockaded our coast, and landed on our shores an army which seized our capital. The success of Jackson at New Orleans obscured the fact that the war ended in a humiliating draw. Similarly, Appomattox and the Grand Review for generations lulled the North (though not the South) into forgetting that the very occurrence of the Civil War, the bloodiest of the world's nineteenth-century struggles, condemned American statecraft on the sectional issue from 1820 to 1860.

Sometimes failure to understand a difficult problem has prevented a true assessment. The passage of the Sherman Act of 1890 and the spectacular trust-busting exploits of Theodore Roosevelt and Taft, for example, were endlessly applauded, although the truth was that for the whole generation 1870-1910 national leaders had little understanding of the forces behind the growth of huge corporations, or of the really valid lines of policy in dealing with them. It is unquestionably true that public opinion has too often lacked both critical edge and expertness. The generally easy conditions of life down to the Great Depression, the pragmatic and intellectually superficial character of most education, and the looseness of the social structure have not favored the development of a critical temper. The hard-pressed peoples of Europe have been more radical in judging the performance of government. "France," wrote Bryce in 1920, "is intensely critical." Britain, France, Scandinavia, and Holland have not suffered demagogues as readily as parts of the United States; they have not excused governmental shortcomings quite so good-naturedly. Our third parties have been our chief critical bodies. The Populists in the 1890s, for example, believed our statesmanship all wrong or at least badly perverted. But such parties have been evanescent.

It may be added that some of the lapses of American statesmanship have been mildly judged because they were failures not of a leader or a party, but of the whole people; and no people is readily given to sharp self-condemnation. The refusal before 1860 to grapple realistically with the slavery problem cannot be laid at the door of Calhoun or Toombs, Clay or Webster. It was essentially a popular failure. Herbert Croly, in *The Promise of American Life,* has stated the record:

It may well be that the Southern planters could never have been argued or persuaded into abolishing an institution which they eventually came to believe was a righteous method of dealing with an inferior race. Nobody can assert with any confidence that they could have been brought by candid, courageous, and just negotiation and discussion into a reasonable frame of mind; but what we do know and can assert is that during the three decades from 1820 to 1850, the national political leaders made absolutely no attempt to deal resolutely, courageously, or candidly with the question. On those occasions when it *would* come to the surface, they contented themselves and public opinion with meaningless compromises. . . . The object of these compromises was not to cure the disease, but merely to allay its symptoms.

In short, the great majority of Americans, North and South, Whigs and Democrats, paltered with and evaded the realities of the dread problem until Lincoln brought the Republican party behind his doctrine that the nation must determine that slavery was a temporary institution, must limit it to its existing bounds, and must sit down to consider just plans for its ultimate eradication. By that tme it was almost too late for a peaceable solution. When the Democratic party broke in two in 1860 and Southern extremists took control, what little chance for peace still existed was thrown away. In Croly's words, public opinion contented itself with meaningless compromise, and the timidities, lethargies, and prejudices of the people themselves were chargeable with the final disaster.

In the same way, the great majority of Americans were responsible for the nation's failure to protect its natural resources from greed and waste until most of the wealth of forests, mines, grazing lands, and waters had been ruthlessly despoiled. This was one of our cardinal failures of statesmanship. Yet because of popular indifference, not until the last decade of the nineteenth century was any effective conservation attempted. Benjamin Harrison, Cleveland, and, most of all, Theodore Roosevelt had to arouse the national conscience in this field. Until 1909 Roosevelt's measures were angrily resisted in the very Rocky Mountain and Pacific Coast regions which they most benefited; and western opposition forced his reform secretary of the interior, Ethan Allen Hitchcock, an intrepid battler against the widespread thievery and fraud, into retirement. Again, all but a minority of Americans were implicated in that dramatic if short-lived mistake, national prohibition. Partly an experiment, partly an eccentricity, and altogether a miscalculation, it was adopted on a wave of wartime mass hysteria.

Just what is the comprehensive record of American statesmanship? While a full answer to that question would require volumes, we may venture a few general observations.

In all countries ideal solutions are usually impossible; statesmanship is a matter of making the second-best choice of policy. Even autocrats know this. "In all your plans of reform," said Catherine the Great to Diderot, "you forget the difference between our positions. All your work is done upon paper, which does not mind what you do to it. It is all of a piece, pliable, and presenting no obstacle either to your pen or to your imagination. But I, poor Empress, have to work upon the human skin, which is terribly ticklish and irritable." Much more does the truth she stated apply to democracies, where human nature asserts itself with complete freedom. The grass-roots variety of democrat in particular is well aware that government is a matter of adjustment among conflicting and sometimes obdurate forces and groups. He knows that political parties in the United States exist rather to unite groups and to compose differences by compromise than to sharpen conflicts.

In large democratic states much more than in autocracies, oligarchies, or totalitarian governments, compromise, opportunism, and blind groping are part of the very fabric of government. Even George Washington had at times to be an opportunist, yielding, for example, to unfortunate pressures toward war with France in 1798-1800. Even Lincoln had occasionally to compromise with principles, as when he got sterile Nevada, with less than the requisite population, admitted to the Union in 1864 to afford him enough votes to pass the Thirteenth Amendment. Even the wisest leader has to use tools that break in his hands, or, as Lincoln put it, "axes that won't cut." All are at the mercy of unforeseeable accidents. Autocrats may have the strength to ignore, at least for a time, great new forces pushing up from below. But the governments of democracies have to recognize these forces, and if possible anticipate them; they have to make sure that evolution takes the place of revolution.

The rapidity with which the American nation developed has meant that forces old and new, traditions fixed and emergent, have been in incessant travail and combat. The colonial era, the period of agrarian expansion and frontier influence, the industial revolution, the epoch of world power, all came in rapid succession. In ancient Rome, Guglielmo Ferrero tells us, Caesar represented the revolutionary impulses, magnificent but devastating, of a new mercantile domination overthrowing the old primitive agrarian culture. Every decision Caesar took in domestic affairs therefore had repercussions that were both good and bad, and often quite unpredictable. Indeed, in the growth of every country the old and new always form a complex whirlpool of elements. The victorious North after the Civil War, for example, adopted policies which completed the triumph of Yankee industrialism over the southern plantation economy. How much that was gracious and happy was lost in the process, and how much that was ultimately priceless in value was created! Later, the displacement of the rugged individualism which Herbert Hoover extolled by the widespread government intervention and welfare policies of the New Deal involved an elaborate mixture of debits and gains. It was an irresistible process, but the balance sheet was long hard to draw. In the choice of policies no first-best for everybody was possible.

But if a broad-based democracy is more likely to deal in second-best or third-best policies than an autocracy, it avoids the fearful catastrophes which the irresponsibility of autocrats has so often precipitated. The most tragic situation a nation can face is that in which freedom of choice is closed and disaster waits on every decision. The France of Louis XVI stood in that position in 1788, the Russia of Nicholas II in 1917, the Italy of Mussolini in 1940. The United States has never remotely approached such a predicament.

The chief disability of American statesmanship has lain in the long antipathy of people and government to planning, and especially expert planning. A resourceful, practical people naturally developed an intense faith in the ability of the common man to do almost anything *ad hoc*, without much preparation. Jackson, devoid of military science, could defeat Pakenham's trained regulars. Goodyear, innocent of scientific training, could stumble on the vulcanization of rubber. Henry Ford could take the sweeper Wandersee in his shop and make him an expert metallurgist. Any militia general could become overnight an efficient congressman, even possibly a President. The half-illiterate Zachary Taylor could make a successful race for the White House without even a party platform. Down to the end of the nineteenth century most Americans retained this faith in the versatile amateur and the potency of impromptu action; they would not cross bridges until they came to them. Not until Theodore Roosevelt came accidentally to power did the day of the planner and expert in government really dawn. His annual message in 1901 was our first clear national blueprint—a very flexible blueprint, to be sure, as suited our instinct for individual freedom.

Yet the greatest triumphs of American statesmanship had been very far from impromptu and amateur efforts. In fact, perhaps the most successful example of statesmanship in the whole history of government in any time or land was also the most striking example of planning and expert effort. That was the labor by which in 1786-89 twelve immature, quarrelsome, drifting states were led to meet in council, frame with wise deliberation a constitution, ratify it, and erect and set in motion a national government. The captaincy of Washington, Madison, Jay and Hamilton disclosed high intellectual power, moral elevation, and earnest industry. From the moment that Madison induced the Virginia legislature to call a commercial convention, and the hour that the Continental Congress under the guidance of Madison, Rufus King, Charles Pinckney, and others, approved the summoning of a much larger gathering, the enterprise was borne forward with extraordinary sagacity, care, and prevision.

The reliance of the leaders on laborious study and design

was indicated by Luther Martin of Maryland. "I applied to history for what lights it would afford me, and I procured everything the most valuable I could find in Philadelphia on the subject of government in general," he wrote. "I devoted my whole time and attention to the business in which we were engaged." The states at that time had at their service a panoply of men as thoroughly trained as they were able. It is not strange that Gladstone spoke of the Constitution as an inspiration, struck off in the heat of a few months, for it so appeared. But in reality it was the fruit of generations of Anglo-American toil and experience, capped by several years of hard work by trained minds. It did not so much arise out of a sudden crisis, in John Fiske's old view, as anticipate a mortal crisis looming ahead.

This was a cooperative effort of leadership, the best and most difficult type. On the personal plane an illustration of the dependence of a true statesman on thought, discipline, and application is afforded by Lincoln. When he reached New York to make his Cooper Union address, many thought of him as a rough-and-ready western orator of uncouth ways and frontier precipitancy. He proved instead that he had a clear, supple, athletic mind which reasoned from first principles; that he had given the history and laws of the country, and the writings of its founders, a more searching study than any college courses could offer; and that he had found an original means of combining profound moral conviction with moderation of temper in lifting the country from the slough into which slavery had brought it. His distinction was not that he was a "man of the people" good at impromptu steps. It was that he had schooled himself to apply rare traits of intellect, generosity, and studious foresight to affairs.

If the chief defect of our statesmanship has sprung from the amateur tradition, its chief strength has arisen from its generally high ethical quality. We have had a special predilection for parties of "moral ideas," like the Republicans in 1856 and Progressives in 1912; we like to stand at Armageddon and battle for the Lord. "The connection between morals, the law, and politics is old and not exclusively American," writes D. W. Brogan. "But in America the connection had been made closer by the religious inheritance of the American people, and by the American belief in the necessity and desirability of legislation to put down manifest evils." Probably a more complex analysis is required, but the fact stands. Nothing in our tradition compels us to ask that every policy succeed. But our tradition has compelled us to ask very searching questions about the ethical soundness of major politics.

Nobody needs to be told how often in history governmental actions that were outrageously bad from a moral standpoint proved to be self-defeating in practical consequences. The Machiavellis and Stalins of this world may score short-term successes, but in the end they fail. We have had the benefit of these historic lessons.

One of the cardinal examples of international criminality was the murder of Carthage by the equestrian order which controlled the Roman Senate. Disarmed, helpless, the great trading city was goaded to rise in self-defense, defeated, and so completely obliterated that a plow was driven over its site. This was despite the patent fact that a prosperous Carthage might have contributed richly to the prosperity of Rome. Another major international crime was the Hundred Years' War. This causeless, useless, and, in the end, hopeless struggle was given by bad Plantagenets to a people who felt no real interest in its conduct; and dearly did both people and dynasty finally pay for it. The support of the Inquisition and its cruelties by Spain stands not more clearly in the category of crime than of folly. The same may be said of the Spanish harrying of Moors and Jews out of a kingdom which was culturally and economically crippled by their departure. Louis XIV's revocation of the Edict of Nantes, which sent 300,000 to his most enlightened and enterprising subjects to neighboring lands, was a wicked act which brought is own penalty. So was his needless and ruthless War of the Spanish Succession, which bankrupted France, slew thousands of her sons, and cost her some of her best colonies. Thus we might pursue the theme down to Hitler and Hideki Tojo.

American annals, despite interludes of cynicism and corruption, present no such lurid instances as these. It is true that the story of our Indian wars contains much that was deplorable. The provocation, however, was often great, the process had a sort of tragic inevitability, and the worst outrages were not chargeable to the government. It is also true that the War of 1812 had a land-grabbing taint, and that the Spanish-American War was almost as discreditable in the way it originated as in the way it was mismanaged. Neither conflict, however, was without real grounds of action, and the second in particular benefited the United States, some insular peoples, and (by the conquest of yellow fever) the world. We used to make apologies for the Mexican War, which research and perspective have shown to be much overdone, if not totally unnecessary. Most chapters of our record expose some inadequate or blundering statecraft, but none lights up an immoral national policy.

We can read the record, moreover, with a sense that the frequent errors have been balanced by numerous instances not only of sagacious statesmanship, but of generosity and forbearance. The establishment of the unfortified boundary with Canada; the repeated adjudication of international difficulties, beginning with the arbitration of the Alabama Claims in 1871; the friendly interest that the United States has shown in the liberation of Latin American nations and the relief of Old World peoples from oppression; the prompt pledges of freedom to Cuba and the Philippines, and their ultimate redemption; the nation's liberal immmigration policy down to 1920, and its long pride in offering a refuge to the unfortunate and maltreated; the many practical applications of the idea of equality of opportunity, and

the broadening validity of the principle of social equality—
these are but a few items in a long list which, with all mod-
esty, we may say proves the existence in America of a
high-minded spirit.

The treatment of war debts by the American government
after the first World War was legalistic, selfish, and short-
sighted. Three Administrations, under popular pressures,
tried to collect some eleven billion dollars over tariff walls
that forbade the shipment of goods. But the lesson of that
futility was well learned. When in history has any other
government forgiven vast obligations so freely as America
did after the Second World War? When has any other nation poured out its treasures of money, machinery, organ-
izing power, and technical skill to aid other peoples so
generously as the United States, beginning with UNRRA,
the Marshall Plan, and the ECA, has done? To be sure,
the motive was partly that of prudent self-defense; but that
a great admixture of idealism entered into the policy nobody can deny.

Happy were the nations which possessed a broad margin
for error, as the United States long had. Our leeway for
going off course and safely getting back, down to 1940,
was not merely the geographical room afforded by wide
seas and friendly frontiers. It was partly economic; we had
reserves of wealth far above our needs, and quickly recovered from what blows we took. While the North defeated
the South with one hand, with the other it developed the
West and linked it to the East. Our margin was partly social. That is, our egalitarian principles and open roads to
opportunity restrained sharp class antagonisms, and kept
painful injustices, such as the lot of farmers and unorganized labor after the Civil War, from becoming perilous.
Our margins were partly psychological, for we had an
American Idea, or, as James Truslow Adams called it, an
American Dream, which at most times commanded a deep
if inarticulate fealty. No doubt we took too much advantage

of our leeway. During the 1850s European observers often said, as they saw northern and southern leaders at each other's throats, that their nations simply could not afford such passions. If France or Britain let herself be divided by ferocious antagonisms, hostile powers would step in to take advantage of the situation.

Now the geographical margin is gone. Bombers with nuclear loads are only a few hours away; guided missiles may cross the hemisphere while we sleep; submarines may rise off New York with implements to blow our cities to smithereens. Our economic margin has been lessened; we are dependent on other lands for not a few materials vital to our security and welfare. The Great Depression for a time weakened our faith in our psychological margin in a way we must not too easily forget. Far from putting our dependence in ourselves alone, we must look for indispensable allies, and make the most of whatever collective security the United Nations may offer. Obviously our statesmanship can no longer be of the impromptu, happy-go-lucky order that distinguished some earlier decades. We cannot have Grants and Hardings in the presidency, Joe McCarthy's in the Senate, and William Salzers in the House without running severe dangers.

Another novel requirement of American statesmanship is that it should now satisfy not merely the home front, but huge and watchful foreign susceptibilities as well. This requirement extends far beyond foreign policy. The Supreme Court decision against school segregation was explicitly approved by some southern editors, who otherwise would have condemned it, on the ground that it was a necessity in setting the United States right before the world. Our national policy toward slums, sweatshops, unions, child labor in industry, public health, education, and old-age pensions was being shaped before world competition between Communism and freedom became acute. But our progressive policies have been accelerated and broadened by a realization that hostile nations magnify our defects, and that uncommitted nations may be swayed by them. This is Jefferson's "decent respect for the opinions of mankind," and Lincoln's warning that American choices affect "man's vast future," in a new aspect—an imperative aspect.

As we find ourselves fully embarked on a new era of statesmanship, we have important advantages as well as grave handicaps. Today we believe in planning; not rigid planning that cramps freedom, but careful forethought. We believe in the expert, so that Washington swarms with industrial, scientific, economic, and military specialists. Our national outlook is larger and more conscientious, if less buoyant and optimistic. But all this is not enough. Back of the sanest and most earnest statesman must stand a sane and earnest people; for it is the people, their spirit, their exaltation, their sagacity, which in the end will count. Highly as we prize intellect, we justly prize character more. One of Woodrow Wilson's ablest advisers, Franklin K. Lane, stated the prime requisite when in 1919, a time of confusion and reaction, he wrote to a specially dedicated friend:

A man who can believe anything is miles ahead of the rest of us. This whole damned world is damned because it is standing in a bog, with no sure ground under anyone's feet. We are the grossest materialists because we only know our bellies and our backs. We worship the great god Comfort. We don't think; we get sensations. The thrill is the thing. All the newspapers, theatres, prove it. We resign ourselves to a life that knows no part of a man but his nerves. We study "reactions" in human beings and in chemistry, recognizing no difference between the two. . . . The world will not move forward by floating on a sea of experimentation. It gets there by believing in precise things, even when they are only one-tenth true.

Chapter 2

Douglas, Buchanan, and the Coming of the War

WHEN JAMES BUCHANAN, standing in a homespun suit before cheering crowds, took the oath of office on March 4, 1857, he seemed confident that the issues before the nation could be readily settled. He spoke about an army road to California, use of the Treasury surplus to pay all the national debt, and proper guardianship of the public lands. In Kansas, he declared, the path ahead was clear. The simple logical rule that the will of the people should determine the institutions of a territory had brought into sight a happy settlement. The inhabitants would declare for or against slavery as they pleased. Opinions differed as to the proper time for making such a decision; but Buchanan thought that "the appropriate period will be when the number of actual residents in the Territory shall justify the formation of a constitution with a view to its admission as a State." He trusted that the long strife between North and South was nearing its end, and that the sectional party which had almost elected Frémont to the presidency would die a natural death.

Two days after the inaugural Buchanan took deep satisfaction in a decision by the Supreme Court of which he had improper foreknowledge: the Dred Scott decision handed down by Chief Justice Taney. Its vital element, so far as the nation's destiny was concerned, was the ruling that the Missouri Compromise restriction, by which slavery had been excluded north of the 36°30′ line, was void; that on the contrary, every territory was open to slavery. Not merely was Congress without power to legislate *against* slavery, but by implication it should act to protect it. Much of the northern press denounced the decision fervently. But the country was prosperous; it was clear that time and political action might change the Supreme Court, bringing a new decision; and the explosion of wrath proved brief.

Buchanan had seen his view sustained; slavery might freely enter any territory, the inhabitants of which could not decide whether to keep it or drop it until they wrote their first constitution. In theory, the highway to national peace was as traversible as the Lancaster turnpike. To be sure, Kansas was rent between two bitter parties, proslavery and antislavery; from the moment Stephen A. Douglas' Kansas-Nebraska Act had thrown open the West to popular sovereignty three years earlier, it had been a theater of unrelenting conflict. Popular sovereignty had simply failed to work. In the spring of 1855 about five thousand invading Missourians, swamping the polls, had given Kansas a fanatically proslavery legislature which the free-soil settlers flatly refused to recognize. That fall a free-soil convention in Topeka had adopted a constitution which the slavery men in turn flatly rejected. Some bloody fighting had ensued. But could not all this be thrust into the past?

In theory, the President might now send out an impartial new governor; and if the people wanted statehood, an election might be held for a new constitutional convention. Then the voters could give the nation its sixteenth slave state or its seventeenth free state—everybody behaving quietly and reasonably. Serenity would prevail. Actually, the idea that the people of Kansas, so violently aroused, would show quiet reason, was about as tenable as the idea that Europeans would begin settling boundary quarrels by a quiet game of chess. Behind the two Kansas parties were grim southerners and determined northerners. "Slavery will now yield a greater profit in Kansas," trumpeted a southern propagandist in *De Bow's Review,* "either to hire out or cultivate the soil, than any other place." He wanted pro-slavery squatters. Meanwhile, Yankees were subsidizing their own settlers. "I know people," said Emerson in a speech, "who are making haste to reduce their expenses and pay their debts . . . to save and earn for the benefit of Kansas emigrants."

Nor was reason in Kansas the only need. Impartiality in Congress, courage in the presidential chair, were also required. The stage was dressed for a brief, fateful melodrama, which more than anything else was to fix the position of James Buchanan and Stephen A. Douglas in history, was to shape the circumstances under which Lincoln made his first national reputation, and was to have more potency than any other single event in deciding whether North and South should remain brothers or fly at each other's throats. That melodrama was entitled "Lecompton." Douglas was to go to his grave believing that, had Buchanan played an honest, resolute part in it, rebellion would have been killed in its incipiency. The role that Buchanan did play may be counted one of the signal failures of American statesmanship.

To hold that the Civil War could not have been averted by wise, firm, and timely action is to concede too much to determinism in history. Winston Churchill said that the Second World War should be called "The Unnecessary War"; the same term might as justly be applied to our Civil War. Passionate unreason among large sections of the population was one ingredient in the broth of conflict. Accident, fortuity, fate, or sheer bad luck (these terms are interchangeable) was another; John Brown's raid, so malign in its effect on opinion, North and South, might justly be termed an accident. Nothing in the logic of forces or events required so crazy an act. But beyond these ingredients lies the further element of wretched leadership. Had the United States possessed three farseeing, imaginative, and resolute Presidents instead of Fillmore, Pierce, and Buchanan, the war might have been postponed until time and economic forces killed its roots. Buchanan was the weakest of the three, and the Lecompton affair lights up his incompetence like a play of lightning across the approaching front of a nocturnal thunderstorm.

The melodrama had two stages, one in faraway, thinly settled Kansas, burning hot in summer, bitter cold in winter, and, though reputedly rich, really so poor that settlers were soon on the brink of starvation. Here the most curious fact was the disparity between the mean actors and the great results they effected. A handful of ignorant, reckless, semi-drunken settlers on the southern side, led by a few desperadoes of politics—the delegates of the Lecompton Constitutional Convention—actually had the power to make or mar the nation. The other stage was Washington. The participants there, representing great interests and ideas, had at least a dignity worthy of the scene and the consequences of their action. James Buchanan faced three main groups in the capital, holding three divergent views of the sectional problem.

The proslavery group (that is, Robert Toombs, Alexander H. Stephens, Jefferson Davis, John Slidell, David Atchison, and many more) demanded that slavery be allowed to expand freely within the territories; and soon they were asking that such expansion be given federal protection against any hostile local action. This stand involved the principle that slavery was morally right, and socially and economically a positive good. Reverdy Johnson of Maryland, in the Dred Scott case, had vehemently argued this very idea—the beneficence of slavery.

The popular sovereignty group, led by Douglas and particularly strong among northwestern Democrats, maintained that in any territory the issue of slavery of free soil should be determined *at all times* by the settlers therein. Douglas modified the Dred Scott doctrine: local police legislation and action, he said, could exclude slavery even before state-making took place. He sternly rejected the demand for federal protection against such exclusion. He would leave the whole matter to the inhabitants; and his popular sovereignty view implied indifference to or rejection of any moral test of slavery. Whether the institution was socially and economically good or bad depended mainly on climate and soil, and moral ideas were irrelevant. He did not care whether slavery was voted up or voted down; the right to a fair vote was the all-important matter.

The free-soil group, led by Seward and Chase, but soon to find its best voice in Lincoln, held that slavery should be excluded from all territories present or future. They insisted that slavery was morally wrong, had been condemned as such by the Fathers, and was increasingly outlawed by the march of world civilization. A few men argued that the free-soil contention was superfluous, in that climate and aridity probably forbade extension of slavery anyhow. But in Lincoln's eyes this did not touch the heart of the matter. It might or might not be expansible. (Already it existed in Delaware and Missouri, and Cuba and Mexico might be conquered for it.) What was important was for America to accept the fact that, being morally wrong and socially an anachronism, it *ought* not to expand; it *ought* to be put in the way of ultimate eradication. Lincoln was a planner. Once the country accepted nonexpansion, it would thereby accept the idea of ultimate extinction. This crisis met and passed, it could sit down and decide when and how, in God's good time and with suitable compensation to slaveholders, the "peculiar institution" might be ended.

The Buchanan who faced these warring groups was a

victim of the mistaken belief among American politicians (like Pierce, Benjamin Harrison, and Warren G. Harding, for example) that it is better to be a poor President than to stick to honorable but lesser posts. He would have made a respectable diplomat or decent Cabinet officer under any really strong President. Sixty-six in 1857, the obese bachelor felt all his years. He had wound his devious way up through a succession of offices without once showing a flash of inspiration or an ounce of grim courage. James K. Polk had accurately characterized him as an old woman—"It is one of his weaknesses that he takes on and magnifies small matters into great and undeserved importance." His principal characteristic was irresolution. "Even among close friends," remarked a southern senator, "he very rarely expressed his opinions at all upon disputed questions, except in language especially marked with a cautious circumspection almost amounting to timidity."

He was industrious, capable, and tactful, a well-read Christian gentleman; he had acquired from forty years of public life a rich fund of experience. But he was pedestrian, humorless, calculating, and pliable. He never made a witty remark, never wrote a memorable sentence, and never showed a touch of distinction. Above all (and this was the source of his irresolution) he had no strong convictions. Associating all his life with southern leaders in Washington, this Pennsylvanian leaned toward their views, but he never disclosed a deep adherence to any principle. Like other weak men, he could be stubborn; still oftener, he could show a petulant irascibility when events pushed him into a corner. And like other timid men, he would sometimes flare out in a sudden burst of anger, directed not against enemies who could hurt him but against friends or neutrals who would not. As the sectional crisis deepened, it became his dominant hope to stumble through it, somehow, and anyhow, so as to leave office with the Union yet intact. His successor could bear the storm.

This was the President who had to deal, in Kansas and

Washington, with men of fierce conviction, stern courage and, all too often, ruthless methods.

In Kansas the proslavery leaders were determined to strike boldly and unscrupulously for a slave state. They maintained close communications with such southern chieftains in Washington as Senator Slidell, Speaker James L. Orr, and Howell Cobb and Jacob Thompson, Buchanan's secretaries of the Treasury and the Interior. Having gained control of the territorial legislature, they meant to keep and use this mastery. Just before Buchanan became President they passed a bill for a constitutional convention —and a more unfair measure was never put on paper. Nearly all county officers, selected not by popular vote but by the dishonestly chosen legislature, were proslavery men. The bill provided that the sheriffs and their deputies should in March, 1857, register the white residents; that the probate judges should then take from the sheriffs complete lists of qualified voters; and that the county commissioners should finally choose election judges.

Everyone knew that a heavy majority of the Kansas settlers were antislavery. Many even of the southerners who had migrated thither opposed the "peculiar institution" as retrogressive and crippling in character. Everybody also knew that Kansas, with hardly thirty thousand people, burdened with debts, and unsupplied with fit roads, schools, or courthouses, was not yet ready for statehood; it still needed the federal government's care. Most Kansans refused to recognize the "bogus" legislature. Yet this legislature was forcing a premature convention, and taking steps to see that the election of delegates was controlled by sheriffs, judges, and county commissioners who were mainly proslavery Democrats. Governor John W. Geary, himself a Democrat appointed by Pierce, indignantly vetoed the bill. But the legislature immediately repassed it over Geary's veto; and when threats against his life increased until citizens laid bets that he would be assassinated within forty days, he resigned in alarm and posted east to apprise the country of imminent perils.

Along the way to Washington, Geary paused to warn the press that a packed convention was about to drag fettered Kansas before Congress with a slavery constitution. This convention would have a free hand, for the bill just passed made no provision for a popular vote on the instrument. Indeed, one legislator admitted that the plan was to avoid popular submission, for he proposed inserting a clause to guard against the possibility that Congress might return the constitution for a referendum. Thus, commented the *Missouri Democrat,* "the felon legislature has provided as effectually for getting the desired result as Louis Napoleon did for getting himself elected Emperor." All this was an ironic commentary on Douglas' maxim: "Let the voice of the people rule."

And Douglas, watching the reckless course of the Kansas legislators with alarm, saw that his principles and his political future were at stake. When his Kansas-Nebraska Act was passed, he had given the North his solemn promise that a free, full, and fair election would decide the future of the two territories. No fraud, no sharp practice, no browbeating would be sanctioned; every male white citizen should have use of the ballot box. He had notified the South that Kansas was almost certain to be free soil. Now he professed confidence that President Buchanan would never permit a breach of fair procedure. He joined Buchanan in persuading one of the nation's ablest men, former Secretary of the Treasury Robert J. Walker, to go out to Kansas in Geary's place as governor. Douglas knew that if he consented to a betrayal of popular sovereignty he would be politically ruined forever in his own state of Illinois.

For a brief space in the spring of 1857 Buchanan seemed to stand firm. In his instructions to Governor Walker he engaged that the new constitution would be laid before the people; and he declared that "they must be protected in the exercise of their right of voting for or against that instrument, and the fair expression of the popular will must not be interrupted by fraud or violence."

It is not strange that the rash proslavery gamesters in Kansas prosecuted their designs despite all Buchanan's fair words and Walker's desperate efforts to stay them. They knew that with four fifths of the people already against them, and the odds growing greater every year, only brazen trickery could effect their end. They were aware that the South, which believed that a fair division would give Kansas to slavery and Nebraska to freedom, expected them to stand firm. They were egged on by the two reckless southern Cabinet members, Howell Cobb and Thompson, who sent an agent, H. L. Martin of Mississippi, out to the Kansas convention. This gathering in Lecompton, with 48 of the 60 members hailing from slave states, was the shabbiest conclave of its kind ever held on American soil. One of Buchanan's Kansas correspondents wrote that he had not supposed such a wild set could be found. The *Kansas News* termed them a body of "broken-down political hacks, demagogues, fire-eaters, perjurers, ruffians, ballot-box stuffers, and loafers." But before the convention broke up with the shout, "Now, boys, let's come and take a drink!" it had written a constitution.

This constitution, the work of a totally unrepresentative body, was a devious repudiation of all the principles Buchanan and Douglas had laid down. Although it contained numerous controversial provisions, such as a limitation of banking to one institution and a bar against free Negroes, the main document was not to be submitted to general vote at all. A nominal reference of the great cardinal question was indeed provided. Voters might cast their ballots for the "constitution with slavery" or the "constitution without slavery." But when closely examined this was seen to be actually a piece of chicanery. Whichever form was adopted, the 200 slaves in Kansas would remain, with a constitutional guarantee against interference. Whenever the proslavery party in Kansas could get control of the legislature, they might open the door wide for more slaves. The rigged convention had put its handiwork before the people with a rigged choice: "Heads I win, tails you lose."

Would Buchanan lay this impudent contrivance before Congress, and ask it to vote the admission of Kansas as a state? Or would he contemptuously spurn it? An intrepid man would not have hesitated an instant to take the honest course; he would not have needed the indignant outcry of the northern press, the outraged roar of Douglas, to inspirit him. But Buchanan quailed before the storm of passion into which proslavery extremists had worked themselves.

The hot blood of the South was now up. That section, grossly misinformed upon events in Kansas, believed that *it* was being cheated. The northern freesoilers had vowed that no new slave state (save by a partition of Texas) should ever be admitted. Southerners thought that in pursuance of this resolve, the Yankees had made unscrupulous use of their wealth and numbers to lay hands on Kansas. Did the North think itself entitled to every piece on the board—to take Kansas as well as California, Minnesota, Iowa, Nebraska, Oregon—to give southerners nothing? The Lecompton delegates, from this point of view, were dauntless champions of a wronged section. What if they did use sharp tactics? That was but a necessary response to northern arrogance. Jefferson Davis declared that his section trembled under a sense of insecurity. "You have made it a political war. We are on the defensive. How far are you to push us?" Sharp threats of secession and battle mingled with the southern denunciations. "Sir," Senator Alfred Iverson of Georgia was soon to assert, "I believe that the time will come when the slave States will be compelled, in vindication of their rights, interests, and honor, to separate from the free States, and erect an independent confederacy; and I am not sure, sir, that the time is not at hand."

Three southern members of the Cabinet, Cobb, Thompson, and John B. Floyd, had taken the measure of Buchanan's pusillanimity. They, with one northern sympathizer, Jeremiah Black, and several White House habitués like John Slidell of Louisiana, constituted a virtual Directory exercising control over the tremulous President. They played on Buchanan's fierce partisan hatred of Republicans, and his jealous dislike of Douglas. They played also on his legalistic cast of mind; after all, the Lecompton constitution was a legal instrument by a legal convention—outwardly. Above all, they played on his fears, his morbid sensitiveness, and his responsiveness to immediate pressures. They could do this the more easily because the threats of disruption and violence were real. Henry S. Foote, a former senator from Mississippi and an enemy of Jefferson Davis, who saw Lecompton in its true light and hurried to Washington to advise the President, writes:

"It was unfortunately of no avail that these efforts to reassure Mr. Buchanan were at that time essayed by myself and others; he had already become thoroughly *panic-stricken;* the howlings of the bulldog of secession had fairly frightened him out of his wits, and he ingloriously resolved to yield without further resistance to the decrial and villification to which he had been so acrimoniously subjected."

And the well-informed Washington correspondent of the New Orleans *Picayune* a little later told just how aggressively the Chief Executive was bludgeoned into submission:

"The President was informed in November, 1857, that the States of Alabama, Mississippi, and South Carolina, and perhaps others, would hold conventions and secede from the Union if the Lecompton Constitution, which established slavery, should not be accepted by Congress. The reason was that these States, supposing that the South had been cheated out of Kansas, were, whether right or wrong, determined to revolt. The President believed this. Senator Hunter, of Virginia, to my knowledge, believed it. Many other eminent men did, and perhaps not without reason."

Buchanan, without imagination as without nerve, began to yield to this southern storm in midsummer, and by November, 1857, he was surrendering completely. When Congress met in December his message upheld the Lecompton Constitution with a tissue of false and evasive statements. Seldom in American history has a chief magistrate made a greater error, or missed a larger opportunity. The astute secretary of his predecessor, Franklin Pierce, wrote: "I had considerable hopes of Mr. Buchanan—I really thought he was a statesman—but I have now come to the settled conclusion that he is just the damndest old fool that has ever occupied the presidential chair. He has deliberately walked overboard with his eyes open—let him drown, for he must."

As Buchanan shrank from the lists, Douglas entered them with that *gaudium certaminis* which was one of his greatest qualities. The finest chapters of his life, his last great contests for the Union, were opening. Obviously he would have had to act under political necessity even if deaf to principle, for had he let popular sovereignty be torn to pieces, Illinois would not have sent him back to the Senate the following year; but he was not the man to turn his back on principle. His struggle against Lecompton was an exhibition of iron determination. The drama of that battle has given it an almost unique place in the record of our party controversies.

"By God, sir!" he exclaimed, "I made James Buchanan, and by God, sir, I will unmake him!" Friends told him that the southern Democrats meant to ruin him. "I have taken a through ticket," rejoined Douglas, "and checked my baggage." He lost no time in facing Buchanan in the White House and denouncing the Lecompton policy. When the President reminded him how Jackson had crushed two party rebels, he was ready with a stinging retort. Douglas was not to be overawed by a man he despised as a weak-

ling. "Mr. President," he snorted, "I wish you to remember
that General Jackson is dead."

As for the southern leaders, Douglas' scorn for the extremists who had coerced Buchanan was unbounded. He
told the Washington correspondent of the Chicago *Journal*
that he had begun his fight as a contest against a single bad
measure. But his blow at Lecompton was a blow against
slavery extension, and he at once had the whole "slave
power" down on him like a pack of wolves. He added: "In
making the fight against this power, I was enabled to stand
off and view the men with whom I had been acting; I was
ashamed I had ever been caught in such company; they are
a set of unprincipled demagogues, bent upon perpetuating
slavery, and by the exercise of that unequal and unfair
power, to control the government or break up the Union;
and I intend to prevent their doing either."

After a long, close, and acrid contest, on April 1, 1858,
Lecompton was defeated. A coalition of Republicans,
Douglasite Democrats, and Know-Nothings struck down
the fraudulent constitution in the House, 120 to 112. When
the vote was announced, a wild cheer rolled through the
galleries. Old Francis P. Blair, Jackson's friend, carried
the news to the dying Thomas Hart Benton, who had been
intensely aroused by the crisis. Benton could barely speak,
but his exultation was unbounded. "In energetic whispers,"
records Blair, "he told his visitor that the same men who
had sought to destroy the republic in 1850 were at the bot-
tom of this accursed Lecompton business. Among the greatest of his consolations in dying was the consciousness that
the House of Representatives had baffled these treasonable
schemes and put the heels of the people on the neck of the
traitors."

The Administration covered its retreat by a hastily con-
cocted measure, the English Bill, under which Kansas was
kept waiting on the doorstep—sure in the end to enter a
free state. The Kansas plotters, the Cobb-Thompson-Floyd

clique in the Cabinet, and Buchanan had all been worsted. But the damage had been done. Southern secessionists had gained fresh strength and greater boldness from their success in coercing the Administration.

The Lecompton struggle left a varied and interesting set of aftereffects. It lifted Stephen A. Douglas to a new plane; he had been a fighting Democratic strategist, but now he became a true national leader, thinking far less of party and more of country. It sharpened the issues which that summer and fall were to form the staple of the memorable Lincoln-Douglas debates in Illinois. At the same time, it deepened the schism which had been growing for some years between southern Democrats and northwestern Democrats, and helped pave the way to that disruption of the party which preceded and facilitated the disruption of the nation. It planted new seeds of dissension in Kansas—seeds which resulted in fresh conflicts between Kansas free-soilers or jayhawkers on one side and Missouri invaders or border ruffians on the other, and in spirit of border lawlessness which was to give the Civil War some of its darkest pages. The Lecompton battle discredited Buchanan in the eyes of most decent northerners, strengthened southern conviction of his weakness, and left the Administration materially and morally weaker in dealing with the problems of the next two and a half critical years.

For the full measure of Buchanan's failure, however, we must go deeper. Had he shown the courage that to an Adams, a Jackson, a Polk, or a Cleveland would have been second nature, the courage that springs from a deep integrity, he might have done the republic an immeasurable service by grappling with disunion when it was yet weak and unprepared. Ex-Senator Foote wrote later that he knew well that a scheme for destroying the Union "had long been on foot in the South." He knew that its leaders "were only waiting for the enfeebling of the Democratic Party in the North, and the general triumph of Free-soilism as a consequence thereof, to alarm the whole South into

acquiescence in their policy." Buchanan's support of the
unwise and corrupt Lecompton constitution thus played
into the plotters' hands.

The same view was taken yet more emphatically by
Douglas. He had inside information in 1857, he later told
the Senate, that four states were threatening Buchanan
with secession. Had that threat been met in the right Jacksonian spirit, had the bluff been called—for the four states
were unprepared for secession and war—the leaders of the
movement would have been utterly discredited. Their conspiracy would have collapsed, and they would have been
so routed and humiliated in 1857 that the Democratic
party schism in 1860 might never have taken place, and
if it had, secession in 1861 would have been impossible.

The roots of the Civil War of course go deep; they go
back beyond Douglas' impetuous Kansas-Nebraska Bill,
back beyond the Mexican War, back beyond the Missouri
Compromise. But the last good chance of averting secession and civil strife was perhaps lost in 1857. Even Zachary Taylor in 1850 had made it plain before his sudden
death that he would use force, if necessary, to crush the
secessionist tendencies which that year became so dangerous. A similar display of principle and resolution seven
years later might well have left the disunionist chieftains of
the Deep South so weakened in prestige that Yancey and
his fellow plotters would have been helpless. The lessons
of this failure in statesmanship, so plain to Douglas, ought
not to be forgotten. The greatest mistake a nation can
make is to put at its helm a man so pliable and unprincipled
that he will palter with a clean-cut and momentous issue.

All conventional treatments of Douglas describe as the
final glorious phase of his career the months in which, as
secession and civil war came, he threw himself with impetuous ardor into the cause of the Union. He pledged
Lincoln the support of the Union Democrats; he would
have made the first call for troops 150,000 men instead of
75,000. But it is not his position in the spring of 1861, fine

as it was, which most deserves praise. After all, every true-hearted Northerner after Fort Sumter was fired with patriotic ardor. We find the most splendid chapters of his life at two other points.

It lies in the Lecompton battle, and in the course he pursued in the last months of the presidential campaign of 1860. Douglas began that campaign with some hope of being elected. By midsummer he knew that these hopes were vain; that the four-cornered election could not even be thrown into the House; that Lincoln's victory was certain. His health was precarious, and his personal fortunes were at low ebb—he was almost bankrupt. Any less determined fighter would have given up and retired to his home. Douglas could have done so without criticism, for not one of the other candidates, Lincoln, Breckinridge, and Bell, undertook a vigorous canvass. But he believed that the Union was in danger. Meeting Senator Henry Wilson in Boston early in August, he predicted Lincoln's election, and declared that he was resolved to go South to urge the people to submit to the result and sustain the government. He was as good as his word. Traveling into slaveholding territory, he exhibited moral courage of the rarest kind by denouncing secession and warning Southerners that if it came it would be met with force.

At Norfolk he told a crowd of seven thousand that no Southern state would be justified in seceding if Lincoln were elected. He also told the crowd that it was the duty of the government to enforce the laws and preserve the Constitution. He himself would do everything in his power to maintain both; and he believed that the next President, whoever he might be, "should treat all attempts to break up the Union . . . as Old Hickory treated the Nullifiers in 1832." At Raleigh, he used even stronger language. "I would hang every man higher than Haman," he said, "who would attempt to resist by force the execution of any provision of the Constitution which our fathers made and bequeathed to us." At Raleigh he also told the South that the

men of the Northwest would never let the lower Mississippi
pass into the hands of a foreign country; before they did
that, they would follow the waters of the Illinois with the
bayonet down to the Gulf. Returning North to New York,
he declared that all true Democrats must join in enforcing
the laws against seceders. "I wish to God," he vociferated,
"that we had an Old Hickory now alive that he might hang
Northern and Southern traitors on the same gallows."

This was a brave stand, for most Democratic politicians
were silent on the issue of secession. It was more—it was a
farsighted stand, for most Republican leaders, including
Lincoln, were scoffing at the idea that secession would
come, while many leaders in all parties were denying that
secession would be followed by war. While such Republicans as Greeley would let the Southern states go in peace,
ex-President Franklin Pierce was writing Jefferson Davis
that any Northern army which tried to march against the
South would have to fight its first desperate battle at home
in the North.

Douglas' greatest single service to his country after Lecompton, was this gallant effort to recall the South, as Lincoln's election became certain, to its duty in the Union; this
bold attempt to warn Southerners that any secession would
mean Northern coercion and war. In that late summer of
1860 he loomed up as incomparably the bravest, wisest,
and most candid statesman in the land.

It would be difficult to find a contrast more striking than
that between the scenes in which Lincoln and Douglas
spent election night in 1860. Lincoln, surrounded by
elated, cheering crowds, went from the old Statehouse to
the telegraph office in Springfield. The little capital had
never heard such a roar as went up when the news came:
"New York fifty thousand for Lincoln!" Cannon boomed;
men and women joined in songs of victory. Douglas spent
the evening in Mobile, at the office of the *Mobile Register*.
To the last he had pointed to the danger of disunion and
the certainty that disunion would inaugurate a bloody war.

As dispatches came in pointing to Lincoln's victory, Douglas sat in growing gloom; not because his friend Honest Abe had been elected, but because he had become convinced, as he toured the South, that a great secessionist conspiracy was approaching its climax. The editor of the *Register,* Forsyth, tried to cheer him. He showed Douglas an editorial calling for a state convention to discuss Alabama's policy in the crisis. The best course for Union men here, he said, would be to accept the general demand for a state convention, elect as many delegates as possible, and divert the proceedings into safe channels. Douglas roused himself like a lion. "You are wrong," he said. "If you Union men cannot prevent a convention, then you can't control the convention once it meets. But Forsyth insisted on printing the editorial. And as Douglas walked back to his hotel through the desolate streets, his secretary noticed that he was "more hopeless than I had ever before seen him."

He was hopeless because he saw into the future; saw disunion and battle just ahead. Hard experience had at last taught him prevision. If we ask which of that night's figures seems the more heroic, Lincoln or Douglas, we must answer Douglas.

Chapter 3

Conditions of Statesmanship in the Civil War Era

1

THERE IS A CERTAIN daring pleasure in putting foot upon a quicksand—if we can draw it back quicker than did Victor Hugo's Gilliatt in *Toilers of the Sea*. Such a quicksand lies in the word statesmanship. If we attempt a definition we shall do well to be ready to leap to the nearest *terra firma*.

As the year 1824 approached, Albert Gallatin looked about to discover some men who, as he put it, "could replace Mr. Jefferson, Mr. Madison, and himself"; that is, for another statesman. John Randolph was too eccentric. William H. Crawford had a powerful mind, inflexible integrity, and a correct judgment, yet he would not do. "Unfortunately," wrote Gallatin, "he was neither indulgent nor civil, and, consequently, was unpopular." John C. Calhoun was pronounced by Gallatin "a smart fellow, one of the first amongst second-rate men, but of lax political principles and an inordinate ambition, not over-delicate in the means of satisfying itself." Henry Clay was a leader of splendid talents and most generous mind, but some doubts could be thrown upon his moral character. As for John Quincy Adams, Gallatin thought him "wanting to a deplorable degree in that most essential quality, a sound and correct judgment." And of Andrew Jackson the great Swiss-American declared that he was "an honest man, and the idol of the worshippers of military glory, but from incapacity, military habits, and habitual disregard of laws and constitutional provisions, entirely unfit for the office of President."

From these judgments (and many similar to them could be adduced) we may infer that no two men ever interpret the term statesman alike; that seldom does a contemporary leader seem a statesman to those who know him best—"Is Saul, also, among the prophets?" scornfully demanded Saul's neighbors—and that if Gallatin could go so far wrong on Calhoun, Adams, and Jackson, we should not be cocksure in our own verdicts.

Yet, as John Locke bade us define our terms, some exploration of the quicksand is indispensable. Throwing down a trial plank, we can say that no *single* test of statesmanship is adequate. The ordinary rude test is success or failure. A statesman is not merely a dead politician, in Tom Reed's famous epigram (to reverse it, we might quote Ambrose Bierce's remark that a politician, as compared with a statesman, "has the disadvantage of being alive"). He is a dead politician whose acts and policies conspicuously succeeded. This *is* the popular test. It was by the test of success that Lincoln fell short in the spring of 1864, when Sumner, Greeley, and others complained that he lacked the essential qualities of a leader, and wished to see the Republican Party nominate someone else. At that time not one of Lincoln's great policies had borne triumphant fruit. His selection of Grant as supreme commander still looked dubious, for Grant had been defeated in the Wilderness. His emancipation proclamation remained largely a nullity until the South was conquered. His effort to weld the discordant parties and factions of the North into a cohesive whole as yet appeared a failure. By the test of success, Lincoln was no statesman early in 1864, and a pre-eminent statesman in 1865. Woodrow Wilson was long discussed in terms of failure, although since the nation has turned back to his policies, his rank as a statesman stands unquestioned.

The fact is, of course, that no leader ever succeeds completely, and a mean success is achievable by any demagogue, while a grand failure is possible only to those with power to try the heights. We may dismiss the idea that a statesman is a successful politician with his bronze hand tucked into the breast of a bronze Prince Albert.

Because even the best statesman can map the future but vaguely, mere luck or fate will always play a certain part in permitting or withholding achievement. Solomon saw this long ago: "He that considereth the wind shall not sow, and he that looketh to the clouds shall not reap." So did Lord Halifax, quoted approvingly by Lord Morley. "He that leaveth nothing to chance," wrote Halifax, "will do few things ill, but he will do very few things." The fortunate leader thus gets praise beyond his due, and the unfortunate man often receives less than his meed. Van Buren and Hoover are lauded while their luck lasts, and mercilessly abused when the skies turn black. The truly vital questions are how high a leader aims, and how much he does to minimize the workings of malign fortune and to exploit favoring winds. The test is not whether a helmsman takes chances, as all men must, but whether, lucky or unlucky, his motives, skill, and prevision were of heroic quality.

And no condemnation by history is more emphatic than that which it gives to leaders who do not take their chances betimes. The odds rise fast against the timid. How they rose against America in the decade before the Civil War! Hoover and Sir John Simon would not take their chances in the Manchurian crisis of 1931, and the odds doubled.

Baldwin and Laval winced before their risks in the Ethiopian crisis, and the odds doubled again. Chamberlain and Daladier retreated once more in the Munich crisis, and the odds had become appalling when the leaders of democracy finally had to take their chance in 1939.

As success is an inadequate test, so, too, is mere ability. Particularly among the English-speaking peoples, who prize the moral element in leadership more than most Continental or Asian folk, and who are stubbornly opposed to the Machiavellian prescription, does ability alone seem insufficient. "Mere ability" may seem a queer phrase, reminding us uncomfortably that the Tory Party hated George Canning for his "damned intellect." Nevertheless, it is a just phrase.

Said the younger Charles Francis Adams in his Lee Centennial Address: "The older I have grown . . . the greater in my esteem, as an element of strength in a people, has Character become, and the less in human affairs have I thought of mere capacity, or even genius." Bismarck is one of the immortals. He wrote his name in history by bold, effective strokes of the highest import. But he mocked at principles, shifted his allegiance when it was convenient, frankly asserted that a great aim justified the ugliest means, and made cynical use of intrigue and deception. What was he but the German counterpart of Richelieu?—and not only do both men seem wanting in moral greatness, but we may well believe that each, because of this deficiency, implanted in the polity of his country seeds of future calamity. Ability is important; but no Aaron Burr, Thurlow Weed, or James G. Blaine attains the name of statesman. Nor, of course, will character unbacked by pre-eminent ability suffice, else we should unhesitatingly call Sir Robert Peel and Grover Cleveland great men.

We require intellectual power; we require moral strength —weight of character; and we require something more— an instinct for the spirit and needs of a critical time. In eras of good feeling and quiet, and in placid, provincial societies, no statesmen appear; and every crisis demands its special leadership, of a type and quality for which the past seldom affords precedent. It is here that we meet the old insoluble problem of the relation between the great man and his environment; the question whether History is shaped by the Hero, or by massive socio-economic forces, or by both. Public opinion is constantly weighing leadership: "New Crisis Puts Solons on Hot Spot," runs the headline. Particularly in a highly articulate democracy is this ever-shifting adjustment between the leader and society of cardinal importance. The Politburo knows how to mold its own public opinion. But in our democracies leadership is dispersed among political chieftains, editors, teachers, writers, ministers, labor leaders, scientists, and businessmen. In a democracy various specialized qualities of leadership find a premium: eloquence counts for much, power of the pen for more, and parliamentary skill, expertness in party management, and governmental experience each have real if shifting values. But above all, the democratic leader needs, in Bryce's words, "the power to comprehend exactly the forces that affect the minds of the people and to discern what they desire and will support."

Gallatin, who is worth quoting twice, said in an address to the New York Historical Society in 1843 that George Washington's special qualities for his crisis were solid sense, weight of character, and an instinct for guiding the people. Washington was not particularly well educated, said Gallatin; he was far from eloquent; he lacked adroitness. But he had solid ability; he had character: "a profound and almost innate sense of justice, on all public occasions a perfect control of his strong passions . . . a most complete and extraordinary self-abnegation. Personal consequences and considerations were not even thought of, they were never thought of, they were obliterated." Above all, he had an instinct for the popular will: "The Americans had a right to be proud of Washington, because he was selected and maintained during his whole career by the people—never could he have thus been chosen and constantly supported had he not been the type and representative of the American people."

An event is a force momentarily made visible; a crisis is usually the product of a collision between new social, economic, and political forces and old institutions and ideas. A statesman then must be not only a leader of ability and character, but one who bears a constructive relation to the emergent forces of his era; forces much more easily defined by leisurely historians a generation later than by hurried practical men caught in the maelstrom which these forces create.

From time to time the fabric and outlook of every country needs a regeneration, and this usually comes about by the introduction of some great new social element into politics. The corruption of the British Government in Robert Walpole's day, and its rottenness, blindness, and inefficiency in Lord North's, were alarming to all keen-sighted men. Many Englishmen despaired of the nation. The situation in France under the feeble ministers and putrescent courts of Louis XV and Louis XVI was still more alarming.

In England, however, the corruption was gradually destroyed by the rise of an active new middle class built on mining, manufactures, and trade, which grew steadily in numbers, wealth, and power, and which brought with it a watchful newspaper press, an outspoken Dissenting clergy, and a body of authors, scholars, and orators who became potent molders of opinion. The new middle class, which was so busy making Britain the workshop, middleman, and banker of the world, had a stern Puritan morality and a deep-seated religious feeling—Quaker, Methodist, Anglican, or what not. The *Times,* the *Guardian,* the *Daily News,* and the other papers had a strong ethical sense edged by the radicalism of Wilkes and Cobbett; the literature created by Dickens, Kingsley, and Thackeray was a

school of practical morals; and the new leadership typified
by Peel, Bright, and Gladstone talked not only a good deal
of cant but a great deal of courageous truth.

In France, the formidable front of corruption and class
injustice sank beneath a different type of onslaught. The
French Revolution gave birth to Napoleonic militarism and
tyranny, with much else that was tragically unfortunate.
But it also brought forward the massive power of the
French people, imbued with emotions that went beyond
hatred of a dead past and pride in martial glory; imbued
also with an enthusiastic faith in man, an exalted if erratic
belief in the destiny of the human race. Before the French
Revolution a statesman of the people was almost impossible; after it came a long succession of them—Thiers,
Guizot, Gambetta, and many others down to Clemenceau.

So, too, in the United States only two generations after
Washington the political system needed a broadening regeneration. It came with the democratic forces of the
Eastern factories and shops, and of the Western farm clear-
ings; and it found its statesmen in Jackson and Lincoln.
Both men were essentially Jeffersonian in temper, though
by no means always in acts. Hamilton, John Adams, and
such later figures as Daniel Webster made the gravest error
in misunderstanding and hence underrating the emergent
democracy of the West; just as Jefferson had made one of
his grandest contributions to statesmanlike growth when,
impressed by the virtues of yeomen, he strove to give
agrarian democracy control of our destinies. The Jeffersonian creed was not highly original. In its attempted restriction of the powers of the national government it was
largely unrealistic, and so ill fitted to the demands of
modern times that in the end it gave way before Hamiltonian principles.

It had tremendous power, however, because it was a
formulation of popular aspirations, convictions, and interests. And as Herbert Croly says, the Jacksonian and

Lincolnian schools were in some respects more Jeffersonian than Jefferson himself, and sought to realize some of his ideas with more vigor and consistency.

Now to divine the hopes, fear, moods, appetites, and opinions of a democracy in time of crisis, a leader needs an instinctive understanding of the masses—a sort of sixth sense which seldom comes without long experience; and to mold public sentiment the greatest leaders need not only ability and character, but some kind of passion. Washington had a passion for independence and union; Jefferson a passion for equality and human freedom; Lincoln a passion for democracy as an example to the whole wide world. Even Hamilton had passion—a passion like that of Cromer in Egypt for governmental efficiency in the interests of the whole people. From passion alone is born an inspired view of the future. The impassioned statesman feels with Wordsworth at Rob Roy's grave:

> *Of old things all are over-old,*
> *Of good things none are good enough;—*
> *We'll show that we can help to frame*
> *A world of other stuff.*

Without passion, a leader may meet the problems of his day with sober practical wisdom, as Monroe, Polk, and Cleveland, strong men all, met theirs. But he can never meet them with inspiration; the inspiration that is the chief hallmark of a truly great statesman like Cavour or Lincoln, Wilson or Churchill.

2

We are thus brought to a question which I have never seen answered, though some kind of answer is necessary to our definition of the conditions of statesmanship in 1861. Why was it that the statesmanship of the Revolutionary era, our first tremendous crisis, was so much more impressive than the statesmanship of the Civil War era, our second? In the Revolution, three million Americans produced a galaxy of Olympian leaders—men who united practical political skill, a firm grasp of basic principles, and a broad vision of the future. Of the first Continental Congress, Lord Chatham declared that "for solidity of reasoning, force of sagacity, and wisdom of conclusion under such a complication of difficult circumstances, no nation or body of men can stand in preference to the General Congress at Philadelphia." Of the same assemblage, Lord Camden wistfully remarked: "I would have given half my fortune to have been a member of that which I believe to be the most virtuous body of men which ever had met or ever will meet together in this world."

It is quite marvelous that Revolutionary Virginia alone should have produced at least four men of truly statesman-like stature: Washington, Jefferson, Madison, and George Mason—a few years more, and we could add John Marshall. Pennsylvania gave us Benjamin Franklin and James Wilson; New York, Alexander Hamilton and Gouverneur Morris; and New England, Roger Sherman and John Adams—to name no more. This is a roster which, in its combination of practical power and theoretical wisdom, is unmatched in the morning hour of any other nation.

How different were the fruits of the Civil War crisis! Thirty million Americans then encountered an ordeal as fierce, dangerous, and, if we include Reconstruction, as prolonged as the Revolutionary test; yet it yielded far less of statesmanship. One transcendent name indeed appears. To most Americans Lincoln seems as illustrious a personage as Washington, and if his figure has less majesty, its spell over plain folk throughout the world is even greater. Their statues stand side by side in the center of London. They are enshrined together in the hearts of lovers of freedom. But apart from Lincoln, the Civil War produced no commanding governmental figures. Whatever the rank we give to Seward, Stanton, and Chase, to Jefferson Davis,

Alexander H. Stephens, and Judah P. Benjamin, we cannot lift them to the plane of the greater Revolutionary leaders. As constructive builders, as vindicators of shining principles, as prophets whose inspiration broods over a succeeding era, they are far less impressive than Washington, Franklin, John Adams, and Hamilton. Why is this?

No doubt numerous reasons might be assigned. It gives us pause to reflect that perhaps American democracy in the period 1789-1860, in raising the level of average political participation, depressed the level of exceptional leaders. As equality gained, so did mediocrity. One main reason, however, is connected with this essential quality of passion or inspiration in the greatest statesmen. The crisis which does most to evoke that divine element is one which not merely calls forth all the energies and talents a people can muster; which not merely renders society plastic and malleable; which not merely ends triumphantly, so that defensive action can pass into constructive action. It is a crisis which seems to throw open the gates to a bright new future for a nation or for mankind; which kindles faith that a refulgent era is dawning. The inspiring crisis has always something of the poet's dream of an hour in which 'twas bliss to be alive.

This was the hallowing character of the Revolutionary crisis. Washington, Franklin, Jefferson, Madison, and Adams were not contending merely for American independence; they believed they were throwing open the gates upon a brighter epoch for all mankind. They began, in Jefferson's words, to "make a communication of grandeur and freedom" to other peoples. "It is comfortable to see the standard of reason at length erected after so many ages during which the human mind has been held in vassalage by kings, priests, and nobles; and it is honorable for us to have produced the first legislature who had the courage to declare that the reason of man may be trusted with the formation of his own opinions." The leaders of the Revolution had faith that they were reshaping American society as an object to all other peoples.

Possessed with an idea of the indefinite perfectibility of human nature, they thought anything possible, and were exalted by the sense that they were participants in a bright new creation. Nor were they wrong. The Revolution, internal as well as external, did create a nation resting on a broad principle of equality, political, social, and economic; a nation where men were to have equal laws, equal political power, equal education, and equal opportunity, as fast as such equality could be made practicable. This was more than a continental achievement. It gave new meaning to human civilization. It made our Revolutionary builders not merely national statesmen, but world statesmen—a fact later registered in Auguste Comte's calendar of great men, and in Frederic Harrison's revision of his list.

Very different was our Civil War. To a great degree it represented a failure of American institutions, reflecting a deeper failure of American life. It was an effort not to open a roseate new chapter in human affairs, but to keep that chapter from being clapped shut. Except in the voice of one man of exceptional power and vision, the war lacked the inspiring note that marked the Revolution. Out of its agonies, losses, confusion, and moral debasement it seemed difficult to create anything ennobling. It was a war not of Construction, but in the words President Taylor's son used for his enthralling war record, of Destruction and Reconstruction—a grim and saddening war.

That the Civil War did have a tragically poetic quality there can be no doubt. It lent itself to memorable poetry written by Walt Whitman, Longfellow, Emerson, Whittier, and Sidney Lanier, as the Revolution had lent itself to prose—to the state papers of the Fathers and the orations of Henry, Everett, and Webster. It was a war of brother against brother, each sure of the justice of his cause: the very essence of tragedy. It demanded mass enlistments of youth, and condemned scores of thousands to lay down their lives with the devotion hymned in Lowell's Commemoration Ode, and the gallantry celebrated in John Esten Cooke's dirge for Pelham:

> *The living are brave and noble.*
> *But the dead were the bravest of all.*

Fought on our own unstoried soil, it invested countless scenes from Gettysburg to Pea Ridge with heroic associations. Lifting Ethiopia to freedom, it had in part the significance of a liberating crusade. It culminated in the martyrdom of the most beloved figure of the century. But if the struggle was full of essential poetry, it was not a war that seemed to open endless vistas of progress and to create a hopeful new world. In great degree, it was a record of the awful penalties of folly, incompetence, and pride.

This was the chief limiting factor in the statesmanship of the Civil War—the tragically negative and destructive nature of the crisis, to which Lincoln alone rose superior. But there were other limitations which we must scrutinize. As I have suggested, American democracy in 1860 did not stand at the happiest stage of its development. Both North and South, but particularly in the largest Northern cities and in the more impoverished Southern districts, power had been entrusted to the masses without a proper effort to educate them for its use. The country had too much illiteracy—a rising foreign-born illiteracy in the North, a sad, though fortunately decreasing, native white illiteracy in the South. Illiterates, and common-schooled but really uneducated voters, accounted for the sway of too many blatant demagogues like Fernando Wood in New York and A. G. Brown in Mississippi. The tone of public morals among those who cheered the Ben Butlers and the Louis T. Wigfalls illustrated a saying of Tocqueville at the time Napoleon III was meeting his first brilliant successes: "The world is a curious theatre, and *there are occasions when the worst pieces succeed best.*" That was true, for example, of some States and cities which temporarily fell under Know-Nothing control, and very true of South Carolina as the Rhett-Pickens school of fire-eaters seized the sceptre.

Then, too, one of the grave limitations upon statesmanship lay in the fact that the country had grown up to face huge and complex problems, but had not yet grown up to the training of experts or the creation of even a rudimentary planning mechanism. The government met its issues *ad hoc,* and often at the last minute with a hurried improvisation by amateurs. No planning was done by Congressional committees. No planning was done by the Cabinet. From Taylor to Buchanan inclusive, no planning worthy of the name was done by a President.

In England, the Ministry usually had to have a program of legislation, and hence had in some degree to mature a plan—although the way in which England blundered into the Crimean War, and the bungling amateurishness with which she fought it, were appalling. In America neither Pierce nor Buchanan ever had a legislative program. The most fateful measure of the decade preceding the war, the Kansas-Nebraska Act, was the work of one man, thrown together in a fortnight, amended in a few hurried consultations, and introduced with no attempt to measure its consequences. The lack of any machinery for thoroughly weighing and shaping policies, and the want of experts to help apply policies, crippled both Washington and Richmond throughout the war. Lincoln, Davis, and their respective Cabinets could attack exigencies with haste and blind energy, and sometimes by a *tour de force* conquer one. But the Presidential or Congressional commission was unknown; so was the unofficial adviser, the E. M. House, Bernard Baruch, or Harry Hopkins; and so was the man who made a true career of government as distinguished from a career of politics.

3

So far as statesmanship went, the ultimate problems of the North and of the South were vitally different in character. This fact, however, was largely ignored in the preoccupation of both governments with the *immediate* problem—that of winning the war. The tendency to concentrate upon military considerations can be illustrated by referring to the most imposing work produced by any Southern leader. Jefferson Davis's 1500-page treatise called *Rise and Fall of the Confederate Government* deserves respectful treatment, both as the product of truly heroic exertions by its author, and as the embodiment of beliefs and emotions poignantly shared by a multitude of Southerners. We need not concern ourselves here with its historical merits, or with its thorough, if otiose, treatment of constitutional questions on which honest men may hold the most divergent opinions. What is here important is the light it throws upon the temper with which Davis approached his task of leadership.

From this point of view, the most remarkable feature of the book is its almost complete silence respecting civil and administrative affairs. The distinguished author says almost nothing of the various departments—State, War, Navy, Treasury. He says almost nothing concerning political factions inside the Confederacy, and nothing at all about the public opinion behind them. He says nothing upon the problem of managing Congress. That his determined application of central controls aroused the most violent dissension, and that powerful groups led by such men as Zeb Vance and Joseph E. Brown displayed the most distressing insubordination, is an elementary fact of Confederate history. Yet Jefferson Davis seems intent on giving his readers the impression that absolute harmony reigned behind the Southern battle lines. The one area of civil government upon which he casts any real illumination is the financial history of the Confederacy.

This silence on civil policy was doubtless in part quite deliberate; the President of the Confederacy wished to defend himself and his section, not to pen a comprehensive history. But in still larger part it was a consequence of his wartime preoccupation with immediate military responsibilities at the expense of political problems and civil issues. Davis always regarded himself a military man. He had been educated at West Point; he had been colonel in the Mexican War, chairman of the Senate Military Affairs Committee, and Secretary of War. In his own eyes, in 1861 he had a larger experience in military matters than any other American except perhaps Scott. The post he would have preferred was general of the Confederate armies. It was almost inevitable that when he became President, a civil official, he should take a much keener interest in military operations than in other subjects; and his memoirs reflect the absorption.

The main task of Jefferson Davis—as he well knew—was not to manage the detailed military operations of the Confederacy; it was to create a Southern nation. He well knew that in order to do this he would have to meet a flood of difficulties, and would in particular have to ride roughshod over the radical believers in State sovereignty. His main task tended always to fall into the background of his mind. Nevertheless, it *was* his main task, and his title to the name of statesman depended upon whether he performed it well.

In making a nation he had to act hurriedly, for his time was short, and to act in a revolutionary situation, which demanded revolutionary measures. For half a century most American Presidents had been administrators carrying out a few simple, well-understood, and manageable policies—and of recent years evading the biggest question of all. Now, in the storm of civil conflict, the Presidents in Washington and Richmond alike had to be bold improvisers—men who understood the cataclysmic nature of the era, and who, within the limits set by public opinion, could lead their peoples in the boldest action and the sternest sacrifice. Davis could make a nation only by showing some of the qualities of the great nation-makers: Washington, Cavour, Masaryk.

The principal responsibility of Lincoln was quite as difficult: it was the preservation of a nation. This meant not merely that he had to find means of bringing the eleven seceded States back into the Union, in itself a task demanding great powers of political, military, and moral leadership. Lincoln had also, while fighting a wasting, bloody war, to maintain the basic unity of a section divided among Democrats and Republicans, Radicals and Moderates, Unionists and Copperheads, Westerners and Easterners—a section swept by a thousand winds of opinion and prejudice, and subject in periods of defeat to terrible ebbs of morale. Preserving the nation meant maintaining at least a fighting minimum of unity and dedication in the North; the unity and dedication that ill-led nations easily lose, as Russia showed in 1917 and France in 1940. Lincoln never failed to realize that this was his paramount task, though he, too, gave more time than was proper to military details. He did not live to write a book of memoirs; but had he done so, it would certainly not have been chiefly concerned with the battle fronts, and would probably have said little about them. It would have dealt primarily with civil problems: with the departments, the Cabinet officers, his relation with Congress, and the civil decisions respecting finance, recruiting, and foreign affairs.

Through it all, we may believe, would have run a single binding cord, the cord of Lincoln's effort to rouse the finest impulses of the people; to teach them that in a successful republic the common citizen must, in Santayana's words, be something of a saint and something of a hero, and to justify Montesquieu's maxim that the principle of democracy is virtue. For that was the binding cord of Lincoln's effort.

Both Davis in trying to make a nation, and Lincoln in trying to preserve one, faced a fundamental difficulty, the lack of cohesiveness and organization in American society. The country over whose division Buchanan had presided in 1860-1861, though fairly homogeneous in blood and language, was singularly invertebrate and ill-knit. Not only was it divided into four diverse sections, North, South, Border, and West, but each section was loose and ungirt. It was to require an industrial revolution, and a revolution in men's ideas as to the function of the central government, to bind the nation tightly together. When Tocqueville published his *Democracy in America,* it was read by many as a treatise on two subjects rather than one. It was of course the ablest study yet made of the merits and defects of democracy, presenting the excellences with glowing cordiality, and at the same time pointing out the dangers to be guarded against and weaknesses to be corrected. But it was also an able study, again in specific terms, of the question of centralization of authority and administration. If we look at John Stuart Mill's incisive comments on Tocqueville's book, we shall see that he was as much interested in the study of Centralization as in that of Democracy.

Like Mill, like nearly all the political thinkers of the period, Tocqueville was an antagonist of Centralization. As a consequence of his observations in America, Britain, and France, he attached high importance to the performance of as many community activities as possible by the people acting as individuals, without governmental direction or help. He believed that only by restricting government within a narrow sphere, and demanding that the collective business of society be done in the main by private enterprise, could the latent capacities of the people be evoked. Only thus could wills be braced, talents developed, and social cooperation promoted. Only in this way, too, could a strong barrier be erected against the chief danger besetting democracy; the danger that, as in ancient Rome, the principal executive officer should become a despot managing the destinies of millions who might be equals, but would be equally slaves.

In the period of Tocqueville, danger of the creation and perversion of despotic central authority existed in France, as Napoleon III demonstrated. Very little such danger existed in Britain. The British realm during the whole generation after 1840 was, as Mill expressed it, a country "where nine-tenths of the internal business which elsewhere devolves on the government, was transacted by agencies independent of it; where Centralization was, and is, the subject not only of rational disapprobation, but of unreasoning prejudice; where jealousy of governmental interference was a blind feeling resisting even the most beneficial exertion of legislative authority to correct the abuses of what pretends to be local government . . ." As for the United States, although Southerners had long worried over centralizing tendencies, and Northern Democrats inveighed against them, these tendencies had yet shown so little practical result that a mere handful of men transacted the executive business in Washington. The central authority was restricted by State Rights, by laissez-faire theories, by the inveterate suspicion of government born in the days of the colonial governors, and by the rapidity with which population had spread over wide areas.

As, in the political sphere, Americans of 1861 had the simplest possible mechanism of government, operated in amateur spirit by men who were amateurs in everything but politics, so, in the economic domain, central organization was almost completely wanting. Corporations were small; associations, societies, and trade unions were weak; no means of mobilizing capital for unified effort on a large scale existed; the sum total of all the men who had any real experience of conducting a large interstate business could have been contained in one ordinary room. The trunk-line railways belonged to the future, for the longest lines, the

Erie and the New York Central, were each restricted to a single State. The corporation which owned physical property in several States was as nearly unknown as the corporation which held stock in several companies; indeed, not until the genius of Rockefeller, Vanderbilt, and a few others grappled with the problem after the Civil War, did corporations controlling a network of interstate interests become a reality. The churches were the only powerful nongovernmental organizations possessing a national character, and all of the churches but two, the Catholic and Episcopalian, were decentralized in administration.

Thus possessing only the rudest, simplest mechanisms, and served only by a personnel of amateurs, the Lincoln Administration and the Jefferson Davis Administration each had to create a Centralized Organization adequate to its colossal tasks. Improvisation—ever more hurried, spasmodic improvisation—had to be the keynote of both efforts. Even the stock of good amateurs was limited. Today we have a surplus of experienced, tested administrative and business experts, just as we have a broad margin of well-trained and experienced military and naval officers; hence it is difficult for us to conceive of the frantic search in 1861-1865 for men equal to their responsibilities. How should the two governments furnish food, uniforms, horses, mules, wagons, cannon, ammunition, for the hosts called to the colors? How deal with the sick, the wounded, the laggard? How coordinate the movements of armies scattered from the Atlantic to Kansas and Texas? And behind these administrative tasks lay the greater problem of welding a national sentiment. How could the two governments bind their respective peoples together materially and morally? Davis, in making a nation, and Lincoln, in preserving a nation, needed all the gifts we have enumerated as requisite to a statesman. They needed the capacity, the weight of character, and the self-abnegation that Gallatin attributed to Washington. They needed the passion, the inspiration, the dedication, of a Pitt, a Mazzini, a Wilson, a Masaryk.

Grappling with almost insoluble problems of organization, confronting a tenacious opponent, and compelled to sustain the morale of their peoples during four years of mounting loss and destruction, Davis, Lincoln, and their associates also needed another quality of statesmanship—patience, patience, patience. Each side had thought the war would be short. The very disorganization of the country made it long. Experts have said that if the national government had possessed a highly trained and fully equipped standing army of 30,000 men concentrated at Washington in 1861, it could have ended the war in a few months. But as the strength of one side grew, so did that of the other. The evenness of the two antagonists in fighting power made the conflict a test of endurance; and the leaders needed all the traits which Tolstoy's *War and Peace* depicts as belonging to Kutusov, who, like Wellington in the Peninsula, by patient, wary, unwearied action finally wore down Napoleon.

March of 1861 found the Lincoln Government, organized on the principle of recognizing in its upper personnel as many Republican factions as possible, at work in Washington: Seward, Chase, Cameron, Welles, Caleb B. Smith, Montgomery Blair—not one possessing any experience in his assigned department. It found the Davis Government, organized on the principle of recognizing in its upper personnel as many Southern States as possible, assembled in Montgomery: Robert Toombs, Christopher G. Memminger, Leroy P. Walker, Stephen R. Mallory, Judah P. Benjamin, and John H. Reagan—again not one possessing any real experience in the department under his charge. The cardinal test of Southern statesmanship, by which we should measure the achievements and failures of Davis and his associates, lies in the question: How much, over and beyond the prosecution of the war, did their ideas, policies, and acts do to create a nation? The primary test of Northern statesmanship, by which we should measure the achievements and failures of Lincoln and his coadjutors, lies in the question: How far, beyond the efficient prosecution of the war, did their ideas, policies, and acts tend to preserve the nation—to consecrate the people to the restoration of national integrity?

Northern leaders did not comprehend the severity of their coming ordeal until, as the army reeled back from Bull Run, the press clamored that the country would yet be undone by mere politicians. Southern leaders did not realize the full magnitude of their ordeal until, as Farragut's fleet passed the lower Mississippi forts, Mrs. Chesnut wrote in her diary what thousands were saying: "New Orleans gone and with it the Confederacy! . . . The Confederacy has been done to death by the politicians." Then both sides girded themselves to meet the deeper tests of statesmanship.

Chapter 4

The Southern Dilemma

1

WHEN JEFFERSON DAVIS CAME to deliver his inaugural
address in Richmond on February 22, 1862, and thus usher
into existence the Permanent Government of the Confederacy, a note of pride crept into his brief recital of Southern
accomplishment. The first year of Confederate history, he
said, had been the most eventful in the annals of the
continent:

A new government has been established, and its machinery put in operation over an area exceeding seven
hundred thousand square miles. The great principles
upon which we have been willing to hazard everything
that is dear to man have made conquests for us which
could never have been achieved by the sword. Our Confederacy has grown from six to thirteen States; and
Maryland . . . will, I believe, when able to speak with
unstifled voice, connect her destiny with the South. Our
people have rallied with unexampled unanimity to the

support of the great principles of constitutional government, with firm resolve to perpetuate by arms the rights which they could not peacefully secure. A million of men, it is estimated, are now standing in hostile array, and waging war along a frontier of thousands of miles. Battles have been fought, sieges have been conducted, and . . . the final result in our favor is not doubtful.

He added some words on Southern unity. "Never has a people evinced a more determined spirit than that now animating men, women, and children in every part of the country." This new national integrity, he predicted, would endure. "The recollections of this great contest, with all its common traditions of glory, of sacrifice, and of blood, will be 'the bond of harmony and enduring affection amongst the people, producing unity in policy, fraternity in sentiment, and just effort in war."

At that time, and for seven months afterward, President Davis's pride and optimism seemed fully justified. To be sure, by that date Missouri had been lost to the Confederacy; the blockade was being tightened all along the coast; Grant and Buell were about to start their advance in the Mississippi Valley, and McClellan to move his host against Richmond. The spring and summer of 1862, however, were in the main a season of Confederate victory. Grant was all but overwhelmed at Shiloh; McClellan's Peninsular campaign broke down in ignominious failure; Stonewall Jackson won in the Shenandoah the war's most spectacular victories against great odds. Lee was able in September of 1862 to invade Maryland, and Braxton Bragg to invade Kentucky. An able student of Confederate history, Robert Selph Henry, tells us that Southern fortunes reached their apex on September 17, when Lee's army in Maryland repulsed McClellan at Sharpsburg, while Braxton Bragg captured Munfordville in Kentucky, thus placing the main Western force in position to effect a swift capture of Louisville and close the Ohio. Their apex—for the tide ebbed as Lee quickly retreated into Virginia, and Bragg was checked by Buel at Perryville.

But, in this brief season of confidence, what were the facts as to Southern unity and devotion? Before the war began a high Southern officer, writing T. C. De Leon from Fayetteville, North Carolina, had declared that he was uncertain of the temper of the Southern people under the branding iron of grim hardship. "When the pockets of the rich and the bellies of the poor are touched they will not be eel-like. They have not been used to being skinned. The crisis will need a pilot at the helm. A canoe and the *Great Eastern* require different pilots."

While Jefferson Davis's inaugural address was still a theme of general discussion, the Confederate Congress passed the first Conscription Act. The law voided the control of the States over all citizens between eighteen and thirty-five, placing them under the exclusive jurisdiction of the President of the Confederacy. In thus striking at the heart of State Rights doctrine, it deeply outraged powerful groups and individuals. Robert Toombs pronounced the act unconstitutional. Linton Stephens declared that it was hostile to the genius of American institutions; that it would "decitizenize" the troops; and that "if the war last long enough under the degrading influences of conscription, they will come out of it utterly unfit for liberty." Alexander H. Stephens termed it dangerous if not fatal. Zebulon Vance of North Carolina burned with resentment, and Governor Joseph E. Brown of Georgia presently asserted: "No act of the Government of the United States prior to the secession of Georgia struck a blow at constitutional liberty so fell as has been stricken [*sic*] by the conscript acts."

Such was one aspect of the difficulty of making the South into a nation, the primary task of Southern statesmanship; and other facets were equally troublesome. Even amid the first ardors and brightest victories, that unity in policy, fraternity in sentiment, and just effort in war of which President Davis spoke so trustfully were hard to evoke; in darker hours they became alarmingly remote.

The secession of the Lower South in 1860-1861 had been the product of varied forces, ideas, and emotions, among which sheer impulse counted for more than is generally supposed. Outside South Carolina, Mississippi, and little Florida it was sanctioned by very narrow majorities; indeed, it may be doubted whether a fair, sober, and complete referendum would have yielded any majority at all in Louisiana, Georgia, Alabama, and Texas. Nor is this strange. From one point of view, the headlong rush of the cotton States to form a new republic may certainly be treated as a confession of bankruptcy in statesmanship. It was rational only on one of two assumptions, both of which proved untenable: first, that the North would consent to the peaceable departure of the Southern sisters, or second, that although the North would resist secession, the ensuing conflict would be too brief for a heavy disturbance of the Southern economy and social structure.

Such men as Davis, Toombs, Iverson, Wigfall, and Slidell, who had spent long periods in Washington, should have known that these assumptions would prove invalid; Alexander H. Stephens and Judah P. Benjamin did know it. And if the assumption were discarded, leaders of the cotton kingdom should have seen that as a means of realizing their main objects, secession was worse than futile.

Secession actually enhanced the peril to the principal ideas and aims for which the Lower South had been contending. The leaders feared a sudden revolution in their social and labor systems; so they rushed into a revolutionary situation which made great and sudden changes unescapable. They feared that slavery would be exposed, after Lincoln's inauguration, to sharp attack; so they took a step which rendered sharp attack inevitable. They believed that the slaveholding regime could be perpetuated only if bulwarks were maintained which kept it in placid isolation from the evolution of Western society; and so they tore down existing bulwarks to expose their society, economy, and culture to stormy change. Even if secession had been peaceable, it would have brought Canada—that is, a foreign refuge for runaway slaves—down to the Southern border, and would have left the cotton kingdom more shelterless against world opprobrium and world pressures. This fact was pointed out by so good a friend of the Deep South as James Buchanan. He later wrote in *Mr. Buchanan's Administration on the Eve of the Rebellion:*

> Besides, they were often warned and must have known that by their separation from the free States, these very rights over slave property, of which they were so jealous, would be in greater jeopardy than they had ever been under the Government of the Union. Theirs would then be the only Government in Christendom which had not abolished or was not in progress to abolish slavery. There would be a strong pressure from abroad against this institution. To resist this effectually would require the power and moral influence of the whole United States. They ought, also, to have foreseen that if their secession should end in civil war, whatever might be the event, slavery would receive a blow from which it could never recover.

"Whatever might be the event," wrote Buchanan, and he was right. For suppose the South had achieved victory. It could have done so only by the devoted aid given by millions of Negro slaves. They had refrained from revolt; so long as no Union force came near, they had remained soberly on plantation and farm; they had been indispensable in tilling the soil, mending roads, digging entrenchments, maintaining railways, and doing rough work in army camps and just behind the lines. And how would the South requite these faithful helpers? That question admitted of but one answer. The fact was that by 1860 the

lot of the four million slaves *had* to be changed greatly for
the better or radically for the worse. In a number of States
harsh repressive laws were passed, and parties arose which
even advocated enslavement of the free Negroes. But could
the South, emerging triumphant from a war in which the
Negroes had been an indispensable auxiliary, huddle them
back into slave huts under the old terms?

By 1863, every thoughtful Southerner knew the answer
was no. Robert Selph Henry calls the stand taken by the
slaves "the highest tribute to the Southern Negro." The
South would have to reward its faithful black allies and
placate world sentiment by a sweeping program of reform
—by protecting the slave's family life; stopping the interstate slave trade; giving him opportunity for education;
and, in short, raising him toward freedom.

The fact was that the shot against Sumter doomed
slavery no matter how the fortunes of the ensuing war went.

In still other areas secession really presaged a defeat of
the aims of the Lower South. What of the effort to maintain an agrarian society with few manufactures and low
tariffs? This, in an independent South, would have clashed
with an inevitable movement to make the new nation self-
sufficient. Davis spoke in his inaugural address of the
progress of a single year, in commerce and industry, toward
"making us a self-supporting and an independent nation."
The Southern Commercial Conventions had laid the foun-
dation for a Hamiltonian program, behind which the pressure of industrialists, bankers, railwaymen, and speculators
would steadily have increased. Georgia would have striven
to become another Pennsylvania, and Louisiana another
New York. An independent South would soon have found
planter and farmer lamenting new strides down the
primrose path toward smoking factories, swelling cities,
protective tariffs, and an industrial proletariat. Southern
agriculture would have hurled the same plaints against
Aiken cotton mills, Birmingham iron foundries, and
Charleston brokers that it had aimed against Lawrence,

Pittsburgh, and New York. Nor would it have been possible to avoid spasmodic increments in national authority and increases in taxation.

The refulgent dream which to many Southerners made all real and imaginary evils worth enduring was the prospect of creating a strong new nation. As painted by Hammond, Ruffin, and Yancey, a republic stretching from Virginia to Lower California, rich in indispensable staples of cotton, tobacco, and sugar, blessed with a harmonious society, and led by a natural aristocracy of talent, would forthwith take a proud place in the forum of powers. Rhett's eloquence and De Bow's statistical fancy described the recapture of the golden age. But how widely was this feeling of Southern nationalism shared as William Lowndes Yancey, welcoming Jefferson Davis to Montgomery, announced, "The hour and the man have met!"? Southern nationalism had certainly made no such progress by 1861 as the feeling of American nationalism had made in 1776.

Even in the Lower South, as I have said, the best evidence is that fully half the population would, in a sober, fairly conducted referendum, have clung to the Union. As for the Upper South, it seceded tardily, reluctantly, and only for very special reasons. It had been divided on the expediency of secession even though it maintained the abstract right, and on the whole was against the step. But when Lincoln called for armed forces to coerce the Lower South—when he challenged the *right* of secession—the Upper South felt it had no alternative but to stalk through the open door. It left the Union because, holding that the States had never surrendered their individual sovereignty, it condemned the Federal coercion of any State.

2

No, in 1861 a Southern nation still had to be made; this was the chief task of the new government; and what were the qualifications of its leaders for the work? The South specially prided itself upon its political leadership, which most men believed to be its crowning glory. Had it not furnished the United States with its greatest Presidents, its ablest Chief Justices, and its most constructive Congressional leaders? Where could the North find names to match Washington, Jefferson, Jackson, Marshall, Taney, Clay, and Calhoun? It was widely supposed that now, in the crisis of 1861, a group of comparable statesmen would take the helm. The election of Davis and Alexander H. Stephens seemed a good start. If the Cabinet unfortunately had to be made up on the principle of trying to give each populous state representation, each state nevertheless was hopeful its own son would play a great role; and Toombs as Secretary of State, Benjamin as Attorney-General, and Reagan as Postmaster-General had the advantage of well-earned reputations throughout the whole section.

Cabinet changes were early and frequent, Toombs being out of the State Department in about five months, and Pope Walker out of the War Department within seven. In all, fourteen men were needed in four years to fill six Cabinet posts. None the less, the Confederacy made singularly little use of some of its most talented sons. Howell Cobb, whose previous career had filled so important a page in national history, held no civil office at all. Toombs proved a misfit in the two capacities in which he was employed, and dropped into grumbling obscurity. Clement C. Clay, one of the South's brightest intellects, failed of reelection as Alabama Senator and spent a barren year as Confederate commissioner in Canada. Herschel V. Johnson, who did not expect the Confederacy to succeed and opposed every centralizing measure, occupied an uncomfortable seat in the Senate. Benjamin H. Hill, who took the other or national side on the principal war measures, held a seat yet more uncomfortable.

J. L. M. Curry had a term in the Confederate House, was defeated for reelection, and confessed that his wartime activities were utterly unimportant. No proper employment was made of the able Robert M. T. Hunter. The brilliant T. R. R. Cobb went into the army, to die at Fredericksburg. Senator Iverson sank without trace, and it would have been better for the South had Senator Yulee done the same, for his principal activity lay in preventing his Florida railroad from contributing much-needed equipment to the vital Confederate lines. Senators Mason and Slidell were condemned to humiliating failure as Confederate envoys abroad, and Slidell remained an exile in Paris after the war—"passing the remnant of a vicious and intriguing career," writes Gideon Welles, "in reading French fictions."

The men who, with Davis and Stephens, played important civil roles in the Confederacy, can be counted on the fingers of two hands. If we listed Judah P. Benjamin, James A. Seddon (the indefatigable Virginian who swayed the War Department in the darkest years of the conflict), Christopher Memminger, John H. Reagan, and Stephen R. Mallory, we should need to add few if any names to the catalogue.

Seven or eight men in all had the task of creating a nation behind the battle lines, and they had to do it with few of the ordinary aids. The development of a national spirit is primarily a moral and spiritual enterprise, which needs every intellectual talent. The South had no poets of the stature of Longfellow, Whittier, Lowell, Emerson, and Whitman, who all helped quicken the Northern pulse. It had no editors so able and devoted as Bryant, Samuel Bowles, Henry J. Raymond, and George William Curtis; indeed, several leading editors, like John Daniels of the Richmond *Examiner,* the Peter Porcupine of the South, and the two Rhetts of the Charleston *Mercury,* were highly mischievous.

It had no clergyman so eloquent as Henry Ward Beecher or T. Starr King. It yielded no pamphleteers so able as Charles J. Stillé, whose essay, "How a Free People Conduct a Long War," was worth half a dozen brigades to the North, or David A. Wells, whose "Our Burden and Our

Strength" helped maintain, at home and abroad, firm faith in Northern victory. The South produced no song comparable with Julia Ward Howe's "Battle Hymn" and no piece of prose fiction to be mentioned in the same breath with Edward Everett Hale's "The Man Without a Country"; and it had no magazine so national as the *Atlantic,* which published Mrs. Howe's poem in February, 1862, and Hale's story in December, 1863. The whole burden of Confederate nation-making fell upon the handful of political leaders.

In administrative matters, right ably did most of them discharge their duties. Judah P. Benjamin had been intelligence, permitting a quick gasp of intricate problems; he possessed versatility, imagination, and suppleness; protesting that he was an idler, he was actually a marvel of industry. Few men dealt with this ever-smiling, ever-polite Israelite, his silvery voice as charming as his cordial friendliness and quick wit, without liking him. Particularly did those susceptible to suave compliments find him ingratiating. He could meet the swiftest change in a situation and cope with the wiliest of politicians.

His luck was bad, particularly in the Bermuda Hundred affair, which caused his temporary downfall, and his best biographer, Robert D. Meade, declares that for two reasons he was a failure in his most important post, the War Department. One reason lay in his unmilitary training and temperament, for the Confederate soldier Alexander Hunter spoke truly when he said that "Mr. Benjamin was a brilliant lawyer, but he knew as much about war as an Arab knows about the Sermon on the Mount." Certainly he never understood the military mind, created needless friction by sharp letters to proud leaders in the field, and harmed some vital military movements by petty meddling.

The other reason assigned for his failure is that he allowed himself to be too largely dominated by Jefferson Davis, failing to stand against the President even when he knew the latter to be wrong in his estimates of men and

policies. Davis came to lean on him for daily companion-
ship and counsel in much the way in which Lincoln leaned
upon Seward, and the counsel should sometimes have been
that of a frank no-man. These judgments, however, will
seem to many overcritical. Benjamin was by no means
wholly a failure, and considering his limited resources, in
both the War and the State Departments he produced
passable results. The two criticisms of him which really
need emphasis are that he had no strong convictions about
anything—about the rightness of the Confederate cause,
about the conduct of the war, about large national policy;
and that his influence counted for practically nothing upon
the South at large, for it never passed beyond departmental
walls.

On other Cabinet members the same judgment can be
passed: they were efficient administrative heads who signally failed to exercise any broad Southern influence; they
succeeded as workers but failed as inspirers. All students
have agreed that in handling the mails Reagan did as well
as could be expected with an impossible situation. Mallory,
the ruler of an almost nonexistent navy, did better with it
than anybody anticipated; his accomplishment, as J. T.
Scharf says, excites surprise and wins admiration. In the
War Department little can be said for Pope Walker, who
began by haggling over prices when the Confederacy
needed every gun and bullet it could obtain, who had little
administrative capacity, who found the demands of con-
tractors, politicians, and army officers intolerable to his
fastidious tastes—"No *gentleman* can be fit for office," he
groaned—and who in general shrank from the rough exigencies of the time.

By contrast, his successor Seddon, despite the ill health
which made him the "walking corpse" of the *Rebel War
Clerk's Diary,* shone resplendently. He had sagacity, insight, and energy. Whereas Walker, as Alexander H.
Stephens said, had been "rash in counsel, irresolute in
action," Seddon was cautious in counsel and resolute in

action. No one can read his annual reports without being impressed by their grasp, shrewdness, and force. Then, too, as an administrator, Memminger evinced industry, devotion, and executive talent. This German martinet had long been chairman of the finance committee of the South Carolina House. Men could almost say of him what Disraeli said of Peel: "The right honorable gentleman's life has been one vast appropriation clause." He proved as good a Treasury head as any man could be who did not see beyond the end of his nose.

All the abler Cabinet officers were hard-working, single-minded, devoted servants to the cause; but not one—not even Benjamin or Seddon—burst from his office confines to rouse to higher zeal the mind and heart of the brave Southern people. Their government was a crisis government, their immediate task the meeting of one long, unending emergency; but they did not have even a Tom Paine in their ranks.

The Davis Administration taken as a whole was open, like all administrations, to grave criticisms on matters of policy. The grand blunder of adhering in 1861-1862 to the delusion that King Cotton could dictate peace, and that Southern interests therefore required an embargo on cotton for the economic coercion of Europe, has been the subject of unending controversy. Memminger, who foolishly thought the war would be short, after it became plain it would be very long, believed in the embargo; Judah P. Benjamin believed in it; President Davis believed in it and encouraged embargo measures at home while posing before Europe as a champion of unrestricted commercial intercourse. But it seems unfair to criticize the Administration on this head in view of the universality, or almost that, of the delusion. Congress, governors, legislatures, newspapers, and nearly every other articulate element shared the belief that if the South withheld cotton from export, Britain and France must in time forcibly smash the blockade.

A more direct criticism can be levelled against Memminger for not accepting the Congressional plan for buying the entire cotton crop and using it as a basis for both financial operations and diplomatic action. But Jefferson Davis was against this plan, and the plodding Memminger was frank to admit his own shortsightedness. Nine years after the war, replying to the strictures of Joseph E. Johnston, he explained that nearly everyone believed that "the blockade could not be continued for a year."

The fact was that, in its delusion as to the sway of King Cotton, the South was largely the victim of its own provincialism. It knew altogether too little of the contemporaneous world, the modern temper, and the new economic structure of Europe. Jefferson Davis was accurate in believing that there would be a cotton famine; he was accurate is believing that the Southern armies could hold the North at bay until this famine became acute; but he was quite inaccurate in measuring the probable response of the British and French working classes to the famine. He did not realize to what effect Lancashire had read *Uncle Tom's Cabin,* or how powerful were the voices of Richard Cobden and John Bright.

Few Southerners had gone abroad, and still fewer had gone as careful students of current tendencies. Most of the South was old-fashioned and behind the times. It read Scott, not Trollope; its literary criticism was based on the principles of Dr. Johnson and Francis Jeffrey; its theology was unaffected by the newer scientific thought; in politics it still liked constitutional disquisitions embellished by the rhetoric of the Honorable Elijah Pogram school. Men truly cultivated and really well-informed as to the contemporaneous world, like Muscoe Garnett and William Henry Trescot, were rare. One alert Southerner, William L. Yancey's brother B. C. Yancey, had indeed returned in 1860 from an English sojourn in which he had diligently inquired as to the probable attitude of Britons high and low toward a slaveholding republic and a deprivation of cotton. His conclusion was realistic—King Cotton's sceptre was mere paper; but then B. C. Yancey found no hearing in places of power.

Equal controversy has raged about the Administration's failure to coordinate the Eastern and Western theaters of military action, and properly support the latter. R. S. Henry speaks caustically of its "usual policy of the dispersed defense of scattered localities," which he thinks was particularly disastrous when it compelled the Western command in 1862-1863 to hold to the bitter end too many river posts, with the result that garrisons as well as posts were lost. The greater error, however, assuredly lay in the tendency of President Davis and Secretaries Walker and Benjamin to concentrate attention upon their Eastern fronts and ignore the Mississippi Valley. A striking contrast can be drawn between the pains the Confederate Government took in the early fortification and heavy garrisoning of Charleston, and its sad neglect of New Orleans, a port far richer and far more important, which was allowed to fall with no struggle worthy of the name.

The Western fronts were far distant: communication even by mail was slow and precarious; ground could be lost there for a time without touching other vital Confederate centers; and not until long after Shiloh was it clear that the Union had a commander of the highest ability in Grant. McClellan's Peninsular thrust demanded the most frenzied exertions by the Richmond authorities. It was all too natural, therefore, to neglect the West. The Virginia front was guarded by the genius of Lee and Jackson, and Charleston in 1863 defended by the high talent of Beauregard; but New Orleans had been left to the politician Mansfield Lovell; at Fort Donelson a divided command was headed by that still more egregious politician, John B. Floyd; and Vicksburg, the greatest fortress of the Confederacy, was entrusted to Pemberton.

Not until Seddon took charge of the War Department in November, 1862, and President Davis the next month visited the West, were systematic efforts made to coordinate Eastern and Western strategy. It is Seddon's chief title to fame that he made determined plans to strengthen the West and reshape its strategy—plans which under Joseph E. Johnston came to naught; and men will never cease to speculate whether the South might not have profited incalculably if the government in May, 1863, had followed Seddon's plan of sending a large part of Lee's army west to help drive Grant from Vicksburg, instead of using that army, as Lee desired, to invade Pennsylvania.

3

But these controversies over policy, however interesting, must not divert us from the central responsibility of the Davis Administration: that of welding the eleven States and nine million people of the Confederacy into a true nation. The brunt of this herculean labor unescapably fell upon one man, Jefferson Davis. Under our American system, the President always gives tone, character, and tendency to the government. An able, resourceful, farsighted President multiplies the faculties of even the ablest subordinate, as a weak President paralyzes their powers. An idealistic President does something to uplift his nation, and a vulgar President to vulgarize it.

Repeatedly we have had Cabinets of all the talents, as under Jefferson, Madison, John Quincy Adams, Polk, Pierce, Lincoln, and Cleveland; but always the question of their effectiveness in national leadership rested with the President. Polk's strong Cabinet did wonders, for Polk had a plan and an iron will; Pierce's still more brilliant Cabinet did little, for Pierce was as weak as he was charming. It was Davis's responsibility to make a nation because the whole South looked to him for that function. Since Calhoun's death he more than anyone else had been the voice of the South; he rose head and shoulders above his Cabinet; he alone could be the Washington of the newborn republic. Would his powers be equal to the test?

Let us do justice to certain rare qualities possessed by Jefferson Davis. The purity and elevation of his character have never been gainsaid. A proud, austere man, his mind luminous if not original, he had the approach of a statesman to public problems. In his prime (by 1861, alas, he was past it) he was a most commanding figure. Seward told William H. Russell that his brains, courage, and dexterity made him pre-eminent among Southern chieftains. His grace and dignity gave him a natural air of leadership, as Carl Schurz, a perceptive observer, records in his vignette of Davis when he was Pierce's War Minister. Writes Schurz:

> He received me graciously. His slender, tall, and erect figure, his spare face, keen eyes, and fine forehead, not broad but high and well-shaped, presented the well-known strong American type. There was in his bearing a dignity which seemed entirely natural and unaffected —that kind of dignity which does not invite familiar approach, but will not render one uneasy by lofty assumption. His courtesy was without any condescending air . . . His conversation ran in easy, and so far as I could judge, well-chosen and sometimes even elegant phrases and the timbre of his voice had something peculiarly agreeable. A few years later I heard him deliver a speech in the Senate, and again I was struck by the dignity of his bearing, the grace of his diction, and the rare charm of his voice—things which greatly distinguished him from many of his colleagues.

The depth of his convictions, as great as Calhoun's, exacts our respect even though we realize that in both men it was allied with a certain humorless fanaticism. No story of Davis is more revealing than that of his sudden heated protest, lying on his sickbed in pre-war days, at the badinage of that other Welshman, William H. Seward, a constant visitor whose facetious humor sometimes jarred upon the Mississipian. The New Yorker had confessed that he often spoke with jocose flippancy. "I *never* say anything that I don't mean!" Davis exclaimed. His dedication to Southern nationalism was complete. Infirm of health, tortured by neuralgia and insomnia, sensitive to hurts that a less finely organized man would have taken in his stride, he toiled with superhuman intensity; and, as a well-trained executive, he showed an efficiency in dispatching business that his great rival in Washington never approached. The South must always remember with special gratitude his magnificent cooperation with Lee.

It is unfortunate that we cannot say more for him, for this service was not enough. He failed to make a Southern nation—that, in view of military defeat, was inevitable; he failed even to make the contribution to that end which might have been expected.

In part the fault lay in his misconception of his true role. The before-mentioned preoccupation of his memoirs— apart from constitutional abstractions—with the military history of the Confederacy, is indicative of this. His greatest ambition in life was military fame, and his faith in his own military genius was so intense that he believed himself the equal of any Southern general. Men who tired of his repeated references to his famous inverted disposition of troops to meet the Mexican charge at Buena Vista were wont to say during the war: "If the Confederacy dies, it will die of a V." His wife records his heartfelt cry, so poignantly absurd, in an hour of desperate Southern peril: "If I could take one wing and Lee the other, I think we could between us wrest a victory from these people."

Jefferson Davis knew in his heart that his main task was a civil task, and not the management of the military affairs of the Confederacy, but he could never quite give himself up to it. A broad oversight of military matters was of course indispensable, but much more of this oversight might with general profit have been entrusted to Seddon and Lee. The frequent interference of Davis with tactical as well as strategic operations; his numerous expressions of personal pride and of irritability in dealing with commanders; his rasping quarrels with Beauregard, Joseph E. Johnston, and others; his favoritism toward the incompetent Commissary-General L. B. Northrop, and to Bragg and Hood—all these acts did the Confederacy a double harm. They often hampered military effort, and they took the President's mind from pressing civil problems. Every student of the surviving official documents of the Confederacy must be struck by Davis's attempts to control too much in military affairs, his approval or disapproval of innumerable orders and reports, and his dictatorial bent.

This readiness to forget his true central role went hand in hand with a tendency, born of stern personal pride, to act not for the current exigency alone, but with a gaze bent to some degree on posterity. When every ounce of his strength was needed for his daily tasks, he would take many hours to write explanatory or defensive letters addressed less to the recipient than to History. An example is the fourteen-page epistle to Joseph E. Johnston just after the fall of Vicksburg (July 15, 1863), which fills most of Chapter Forty-two in Mrs. Davis's second volume. Davis seems to have been right, Johnston wrong; but was this formidably quarrelsome letter worth while with so much to be done? To quarrel at all was a mistake; for as Plutarch says, "Anger turns the mind out of doors and bolts the door"—that is, it interferes with clear thinking.

The results of Davis's misapplication of energy and temper soon became evident. For him, as for Lincoln, a critical election came midway in the war. Lincoln held his ground in 1862, keeping control of Congress; had he not done so, the North might well have lost the war. Davis, defeated in the Congressional elections of 1863, saw the legislative branch taken over by a hostile majority. Perhaps even the strongest and most tactful of Presidents could not have rallied a united South after Vicksburg and Gettysburg. Nevertheless, Davis combined a remarkable capacity for making foes with a remarkable incapacity for mobilizing friends.

The roster of his opponents became terrifying: Rhett, Yancey, Wigfall, Henry S. Foote, Beauregard, Joseph E. Johnston, Vance, Stephens, Joseph E. Brown, Yulee, Herschel Johnson, and many more. Some of them denounced Davis more savagely than the government in Washington. "Timid, peevish, and obstinate," wrote Stephens. The distilled venom of these enemies may be found sealed into the pages of Edward A. Pollard's *The Lost Cause*. It would be hard to name a worse piece of pseudo-history than Pollard's, a book so bad from every point of view that it should never have been published. It is not history but prejudiced and mean-spirited gossip. But it is surely significant that a volume so abusive of Jefferson Davis appeared just after the close of the war, and quickly found millions of readers. Still more significant are the scarifying passages upon him as viewed by the private soldiers in George Cary Eggleston's *A Rebel's Recollections;* "the grand master of incapacity," writes Eggleston. He had lost touch—sympathetic touch—with public opinion. By 1865, states R. W. Patrick in *Jefferson Davis and His Cabinet,* "perhaps half of his countrymen had little use for Davis and his Administration."

Varina Howell Davis, in her admirable work on her husband, admits this loss of control over public sentiment, attributing his growing unpopularity to the fact that ill-health forbade him to receive many people, entertain, or show himself much in public. "He was a nervous dyspeptic"; "he said he could do one duty or the other—give entertainments or administer the Government"; "in the evening he was too exhausted to receive informal visitors." She thinks that had he been physically equal to frequent meetings with Congress, the Virginia officials, and the people, his magnetism would have "mollified their resentments." Yet at the same time she admits that his magnetism was seldom visible. "He was abnormally sensitive to disapprobation . . . He felt how much he was misunderstood, and the sense of mortification and injustice gave him a repellent manner." Ill-health was no doubt part of the explanation—but the essential nature of the man was deeply involved.

His very real distinction of mind and manner, we feel, was built on too narrow a basis; his fine nature was too reserved, his elevated character too aristocratic. It could be said of him as of the second Pitt: "He never grew—he was cast." He was too intense and keen-edged, or, to use W. H. Russell's term, too drastic. In this respect he contrasted with the Illinoisan whose rich personality, wrote Lowell, offered no lonely mountain-peak of mind,

> *Broad prairie rather, genial, level-lined,*
> *Fruitful and friendly for all human-kind,*

and who won the increasing affection of the democratic masses. Mr. Douglas Freeman tells me that Robert E. Lee, viewing Abraham Lincoln across the battle lines, had the picture of a leader endowed with illimitable patience; that it was Lincoln's sagacious patience and persistence which gave Lee a touch of dread. Mr. Freeman also says that if he were asked to identify the primary trait which enabled Washington to carry the nation through the Revolution, he would name this identical quality of patience. The maker of the nation and its preserver were alike endowed with two magic gifts, utter self-abnegation and utter patience; gifts closely linked, for the man who thinks of self-interest cannot be patient.

The impracticable element in Davis's temper is revealed in his relations with Congress and Cabinet. He vetoed no fewer than thirty-nine acts of Congress, proof of the friction between its leaders and himself. Lincoln meanwhile, plagued by an equally factious Congress, went to the greatest lengths to avoid vetoes. He abandoned a contemplated veto of the Second Confiscation Act, knowing that the law would have meaning only as he and his Attorney-General enforced it. He gave only a pocket veto to the Wade-Davis bill on reconstruction, which he detested, and then took care to muster public sentiment behind himself in one of those closely argued appeals to reason which he knew so well how to write. Among the harshest critics of his policies was Charles Sumner; Lincoln made the difficult Massachusetts Senator an intimate friend, always welcome at the White House. When Sumner by a particularly mean-spirited maneuver thwarted one of Lincoln's dearest projects, the President sent him a note asking him to ride in his carriage to the second inauguration! We well know what Davis would have done in such circumstances.

As for Cabinet relations, Lincoln made but four changes in his official family, as against Davis's eight, and two of these were hardly chargeable to him; for the incompetent Cameron and lackadaisical Caleb B. Smith had gotten into the Cabinet as a result of pre-convention bargains made by David Davis and Leonard Swett behind Lincoln's back, and both in time were glad to get out. Lincoln prevented Congress from forcing Cabinet changes, even when in the crisis after Fredericksburg the most fearful assault was made on Seward. Davis, however, consented to the departure of Memminger and Seddon under fire, and even the sympathetic Professor Patrick, in treating the controversy with a Congressional group which led to Seddon's resignation, writes that the President's jealousy of his own dignity and want of tact were chiefly responsible. Reagan, Benjamin, and Seddon had much to say in praise of Davis when they retired. But they could never have uttered the immortal tribute which the long-surly Stanton paid to the President coffined in the East Room: "There lies the greatest master of men who ever lived."

But the principal deficiency of Davis as a nation-maker, the respect in which he most clearly falls behind Cavour, Masaryk, and Gandhi, lay in his want of passion. The great nation-builder must have some of the qualities of seer and poet, as these strong nationalists had; as even Bismarck, in his rough way, had. All these men could profoundly stir and inspire the hearts of their people. In his four years in Washington, Lincoln touched again and again the highest emotions of his countrymen. When did Davis, for all his devotion to a great cause, ever do it? He had a reputation for eloquence, but it was an eloquence cold, chiselled, and intellectual. Why was it that the winged words always came from the other side of the Potomac?

"Fellow citizens, *we* cannot escape history. We, of this Congress and this Administration, will be remembered in spite of ourselves . . . The fiery trial through which we pass will light us down, in honor or dishonor, to the latest generation . . . We shall nobly save, or meanly lose, the last best hope of earth." What Congress would not be inspired by such an admonition? "General, I have heard, in such a way as to believe it, of your recently saying that both the army and the government needed a dictator. Of course, it was not for this, but in spite of it, that I have given you the command. Only those generals who win successes can set up as dictators. What I now ask of you is military success, and I will risk the dictatorship. The government will support you to the utmost of its ability . . . And now, beware of rashness. Beware of rashness, but, with energy and sleepless vigilance, go forward and give us victories." What general would not do his utmost after such an appeal? "Still, let us not be over-sanguine of a speedy final triumph. Let us be quite sober. Let us diligently apply the means, never doubting that a just God, in his own good time, will give us the rightful result." What citizen would not be more patient after that advice?

Such works, like those of Churchill in the last war, come only from a vision, generosity, and insight which were not in the devoted and heroic Davis. We cannot see how the South could have had grander generals than Lee and Stonewall Jackson, but we can easily see how it might have had a greater civil leadership.

4

Yet it would be unjust to lay the main responsibility for a want of passion and inspiration upon the deficiencies of Davis and his colleagues. The final reason why this Administration exhibited so little of these qualities lies deeper than any personal limitation.

The South faced two great dilemmas. One, which has been treated so fully by historians that it is unnecessary to dwell upon it, was the practical political choice between State Rights and far-reaching, drastic measures for the survival of the Confederacy. Dr. Frank L. Owsley, examining what he calls the seamy side of Southern history in *State Rights in the Confederacy*, concludes that the South failed not because of overwhelming Northern strength, not because of the blockade, not because of any other external factor, but because of internal weakness. The seeds of death were implanted in the Confederacy at birth, he states, and these seeds were State Rights.

Jefferson Davis was an unyielding nationalist, loyal to the South rather than to Mississippi, ready to consolidate the Confederacy at the cost of State privileges, and bold in his strokes for independence no matter how angrily governors protested at some of them. He offended Governor Brown of Georgia, who was concerned with the defense of Georgia no matter what happened to Virginia or Tennessee; he outraged Governor Vance of North Carolina; he provoked Governor Milton of Florida to declare that he would rather see his State a desert drenched with the blood of its people than a vassal to Richmond. The first quarrel was over arms; had the States given them up freely to the new nation, the Confederacy might have equipped 600,000 instead of 400,000 soldiers by the end of 1861. A fiercer quarrel followed over the conscription of men; the States always kept large forces for local defense—perhaps an average of 100,000 much needed troops in 1862-1863.

The bitter competition of the Confederacy and the States for vital supplies was meanwhile never ended; and when Lee's half-naked army fought its last battles with Grant, Governor Vance had 92,000 untouched uniforms in North Carolina depots.

The other and greater Southern dilemma was moral in character; and in it lies the principal reason why the Jefferson Davis Administration could never display the passion —the moral earnestness—which we find in Washington and Bolívar, Mazzini and Masaryk. The Confederacy emerged as a paladin of the ideas of freedom and self-determination. It also emerged as a great slaveholding nation; in Buchanan's words, the one important government in Christendom which had not abolished or was not in progress to abolish slavery. On the one side, it fought for a noble ideal of liberty; on the other, for the institution of servitude. It stood in an equivocal position on the world stage. Gladstone said: "There is no war except one, the war for liberty, that does not contain in it elements of corruption as well as of misery."

A thoughtful Southerner, Nathaniel W. Stephenson, wrote some years ago that the South had hopelessly compromised itself in not taking action, ten or fifteen years before 1861, to convert slavery into serfdom. Certainly it faced a crippling moral dilemma just after secession. For if it hoped to foster widespread foreign support, or to stimulate its own advanced and idealistic elements to desperate exertions, it must promise a grand amelioration of slavery, while if it made such a promise—as not a few voices even in 1861 demanded—it would hopelessly offend those who, like R. M. T. Hunter, exclaimed: "What did we secede for if not to save our slaves?"

Everyone is familiar with the protestation, "The Confederacy did not fight for slavery"; the argument, "Slavery was the occasion, not the cause, of the war"; and the question, "How could slavery have been the main issue when so heavy a majority of Southerners had no slaves and wanted none?" We all know that Robert E. Lee emancipated his slaves and pronounced slavery a misfortune; that Stonewall Jackson never owned but two slaves and gave both an opportunity to earn their freedom; that Joseph E. Johnston never had a slave and disliked the institution; that Matthew Fontaine Maury termed slavery a curse; and that A. P. Hill never had a slave and thought slavery a deplorable evil.

Unhappily, it is equally true that when the Confederacy was created many Southerners expected to bulwark and extend slavery. In the first Congress some designing men introduced a bill for reviving the slave trade; that is, providing that if a slave ship were "wrecked" on the Southern coast, the Negroes were to be sold at auction. Alexander H. Stephens's famous cornerstone speech was received with acclamation in much of the South, as with hot condemnation in much of the North and of Europe. "Our new government," he said, "is founded upon the opposite idea [to that of the Declaration of Independence]; its foundations are laid, its cornerstone rests, upon the great truth that the Negro is not equal to the white man, that slavery —subordination to the superior race—is his natural and normal condition . . . This stone which was rejected by the first builders, is become the chief stone of the corner in our new edifice."

The basic attitudes of the South toward slavery of course form much too complex a subject for brief analysis. It would perhaps be roughly fair to say, however, that the more enlightened Southerners were fighting for the right to deal with the joint problems of slavery and race adjustment in their own time and on their own terms. Most informed men realized that slavery was not an institution which would last forever; that soon it would have to be modified, and eventually, relinquished. They knew that the South could not maintain it very long after it ceased to serve a useful economic and social service, and that its utility was nearing an end. They wished, however, to choose the hour and method by which they should decree its gradual extinction. Knowing the complexity of the problem, they did not desire to be whirled into a catastrophic social revolution.

Why, we may ask, did the Confederate leaders not say this? If they announced that the new nation regarded slavery as a transitional system, and would soon study plans for abolishing the internal slave trade, legalizing slave marriages, and providing education for slave children, a host of Europeans might have moved to their side. "See," conservative Britons and Frenchmen might have said, "the Southern republic already goes beyond anything the North has dared to propose." Still more important, an announcement of this policy would have accentuated the Northern divisions. Even as it was, the Copperheads formed a powerful body, and the Laodiceans were numerous. Strengthened by such a pronouncement, the disloyal, the peace-loving, and the faint-hearted might, as Lee continued to win victories, have become irresistible.

But, in the light of thirty years of Southern defensiveness, the obstacles before so bold a step seemed insuperable. An announcement sufficiently strong to impress public opinion abroad and in the North would have shaken the Lower South to its foundations. There came a time when a more reckless, more desperate, or more convinced Confederate Government might really have acted. After Chickamauga in 1863, General Patrick Cleburne, appalled by the depletion of Southern ranks and the difficulty of obtaining recruits for the Western forces, prepared a careful paper advising the emancipation and enlistment of slaves. Letters in the Bragg Collection at the Western Reserve Historical Society show that this paper was signed by Generals Hardee, Polk, Cheatham, Hindman, and others.

Bragg himself referred to it as representing an "abolitionist" movement and as sponsored by the new "Abolition Party of the South." When early in 1864 it found its way by an unfriendly hand to Davis, he wrote that he appreciated the patriotic motive of the fourteen officers who had signed it, but that it was impolitic to make so controversial a document public, and he wished it suppressed. He knew that any decided step in that direction would split the South asunder. At this time even so mild an interference with slavery as the attempt of the Confederate Government to impress 20,000 slaves for labor purposes aroused the bitterest resentment. Governor Vance flatly rejected the national requisition, while South Carolina and Florida passed laws which practically nullified the Confederate statute.

The South was the prisoner of its dilemma. The one course Davis and his associates felt able to take was to remain silent—and silence implied the rejection of a constructive policy. Throughout the war the frozen taciturnity of Davis, Stephens, Benjamin and others on slavery gave Europe and the North no option but to believe that Confederate victory would mean the perpetuation of the institution; nay, would probably mean its extension over adjacent Caribbean areas. The government's blunder in sending Yancey as its envoy to England helped confirm that view, for England knew Yancey as an arch-defender of slavery and an advocate of reviving the slave trade. John Bright scornfully repeated Stephens's cornerstone declaration in Exeter Hall. Goldwin Smith, the Duke of Argyll, Cairnes, John Stuart Mill and other sympathizers with the North made the most of similar proslavery utterances. As discussion of slavery had been tabu in the South before the war, so now it remained the skeleton locked in the closet.

Between the Scylla of world opinion and the Charybdis of Southern pride, sensitiveness, and economic interest, Confederate statesmanship stood immobile. Eventually it went to shipwreck on both. By the end of 1863 all hope of foreign intervention was gone, and by the beginning of September, 1864, all chance of Democratic victory in the North was ended. Yet the movement for the enlistment (and emancipation) of slaves had, without governmental encouragement, taken on strength. Late in 1864 General Lee was converted to it. Jefferson Davis himself finally came over. In a message of November 7, 1864, he proposed enlisting 40,000 Negroes for service, with a grant of freedom to all willing fighters. He also expressed doubt whether "the private right of property [in human beings] can consistently and beneficially be continued."

But desperate as the Confederate position had then become, the stand of Davis and the still bolder activities of Benjamin provoked a wild storm. When Benjamin at the famous meeting held at the African Church in Richmond on February 9, 1865, proposed a general enlistment of Negro soldiers, with the promise, "You are free," his doctrine was denounced as revolutionary, and Wigfall introduced in Congress a resolution that the country had lost confidence in him.

Years after the war ended Judah P. Benjamin walked home from a Mayfair dinner party with William H. Russell. The journalist reminded the Southern exile that, when Attorney-General in Montgomery, he had predicted that within a year Britain would break the blockade. "When your factories are closed," Benjamin had then said, in effect, "when the Mississippi is floating cotton by thousands of bales, and all our wharves are full, it is inevitable that the Yankees will come to grief in the effort to coerce us." Russell, as the two strolled down Park Lane, spoke of the failure of the prophecy. "Ah, yes," responded Benjamin. "I was mistaken. I did not believe that your government would allow such misery to be visited on your workers, such loss to be inflicted on your manufacturers. I did not believe the people would have borne it."

The Lancashire operatives had borne it because of the weight of moral imponderables. They would not lend their support to a great slaveholding nation. They had pondered *Uncle Tom's Cabin*. They knew something of the history of the British antislavery movement. Their spokesmen in Parliament were Cobden, Bright, and Forster. And although their wives were ragged and their children hungry, they were on the side of human freedom. So it was with certain wavering segments of Northern opinion. Not least among the decisive battles of the war was this struggle for the control of British and Northern opinion, and not the smallest of the Northern victories was that won in the streets of Lancashire and at the Northern polling places.

The Southern republic indeed had the seeds of death implanted in it at birth. But there were two kinds of seeds —State Rights and slavery; and of the two slavery was the more important, for it deprived Southern statesmanship of all chance of expressing that passion, that soul-stirring inspiration which alone could make the new nation invincible and raise up friends for it beyond its borders.

If we look for inspiration, we find it, not in the council-chambers of the Confederacy, but on the battlefields; not in Davis, admirable as were some of his qualities, but in Lee and Jackson. In the end the two greatest acts of statesmanship were performed by Robert E. Lee. These acts of statesmanship were indeed among the most notable in all American history. When, after the fall of Richmond, it was proposed to Lee that he withdraw southward, take command of troops still available there, and conduct a protracted guerrilla resistance to the North, he had the statesmanlike vision and courage to refuse. He knew that such an effort to fight to the last ravine and last range of mountains would mean incalculable misery to the South as well as heavy loss to the North; that it would to no good end prolong the sorrows and intensify the bitterness of the conflict. Later still, it was Lee who did most to set a manly example of loyalty to the restored Union, and constructive labor for the rehabilitation of war-strained society. As the figure of Lincoln the statesman disappeared from the national stage, the figure of Lee the statesman momentarily appeared upon it.

Chapter 5

Lincoln's Ideas of Democracy

IT IS AN INCONTESTABLE FACT that Americans in their first century of independence did little intensive thinking upon democracy. They accepted its existence and its beneficence upon faith. Our first formal treatise on the subject was a book published by Charles Camp in 1836 entitled *Democracy,* and he lamented this lack of intensive thinking.* Americans, he wrote, were content to live "in the rich experience and practical enjoyment of democratic freedom, but in entire and reckless indifference to its abstract principles." No native school of philosophers had arisen to combat the hostile European theorists then so numerous. Americans surrendered the field to Tocqueville, the first part of whose *La Démocratie en Amérique* appeared in 1835, and the second in 1840.

Why this neglect? For one reason, because the pragmatic bent of Americans made them satisfied with the "rich experience"; why theorize upon it? For another, noted by Harriet Martineau, the ideas of the Declaration of Inde-

* The author owes the quotation from Camp to a writer in the *New England Quarterly.*

97

pendence took the place of an explicit rationale of democracy. This great document was the milk of the word. Its twin principles of faith in natural law, and faith in the indefinite perfectibility of man, underlay our scheme of government and society, and could be expanded to cover the whole American future. And finally, the history of party tenets was believed to furnish a good theoretical framework for American political thinking. Study the party conflict, they said, and you would understand the nature of American democracy.

When Henry Adams wrote his novel *Democracy,* he too commented upon this vague, inarticulate attitude toward the subject. Early in the book, that epitome of Congressional coarseness whom he calls Senator Ratcliffe, standing in a Washington drawing room, asserts his belief that the reform of government must wait upon the reform of the people. "Purify society and you purify the government. But try to purify the government artificially and you only aggravate failure." This sneer at reformers brings from a foreign member of the group, Baron Jacobi, a statement that he had never seen a society which possessed so many elements of corruption as the United States. Thereupon Mrs. Lightfoot Lee, the hostess, interposes to ask Mr. Gore, a historian, what *he* thinks of Ratcliffe's ideas about the people. "Do you yourself," she inquires, "think democracy the best government, and universal suffrage a success?" Poor historian! He wriggles hopelessly, for he, too, has never really thought about democracy. But he must answer, and he finally turns at bay with something like despair.

"These are matters," he says, "about which I rarely talk in society; they are like the doctrine of a personal God; of a future life; of revealed religion; subjects which one naturally reserves for private reflection. But since you ask for my political creed you shall have it . . . never to be repeated or quoted as mine. I believe in democracy. I accept it. I will faithfully serve it. I believe in it because it appears to me the inevitable consequence of what has gone before it. Democracy asserts the fact that the masses are now raised to a higher level of intelligence than formerly." Having floundered that far, he stopped; he had nothing more to say about democracy.

It must be admitted that, like his fellow countrymen, Lincoln made few and limited statements of an abstract character upon democracy; he took it on faith, without analysis. Political democracy, to him, was the rule of the people; and he declared again and again that he believed in the virtue and strength of the whole people whenever they were properly instructed. God must have loved the people, he said, or He would not have made so many of them; you could never fool all of the people all of the time; government of, for, and by the people was not only the best government, but the hope of the world. In contradistinction to John Adams, whose sympathies were with an elite, he liked to speak of the plain people, meaning everyday citizens who were like himself in not having much property or much formal education.

Out of this deep regard for the common folk came Lincoln's seldom-erring instinct for popular sentiment; he divined how far and how fast he could go without losing touch with the majority. Out of it came his consistent refusal to talk down to the people, or to appeal to their passions. As Lowell wrote, he never played the Cleon—the demagogue. Instead, he presented the people with careful arguments, addressed to their reason and their loftier instincts. "I beg of you," he once said, after listing a certain set of arguments, "a calm and enlarged consideration of them." On minor questions he believed the people could err grievously; but on fundamental issues he would trust them, in the end, to decide aright. Perhaps the greatest decision they had to make in his time was that registered in the election of 1864, when they might have rejected him and his administration, and given up the Union in favor of immediate peace. He knew they would not flinch, and they did not. As he wrote just after the election:

> The purpose of the people within the loyal States to maintain the integrity of the Union was never more firm nor more nearly unanimous than now. The extraordinary calmness and good order with which the millions of voters met and mingled at the polls give strong assurance of this. . . . There have been much impugning of motives, and much heated controversy as to the proper means and best mode of advancing the Union cause; but on the distinct issue of Union or no Union the politicians have shown their instinctive knowledge that there is no diversity among the people. In affording the people the fair opportunity of showing one to another and to the world this firmness and unanimity of purpose, the election has been of vast value to the national cause.

Instead of discoursing on the theory of democracy, Lincoln preferred to speak of its purposes, its significance, its perils, and its successes; that is, of the practical problems attending its course. Its main purpose, often obscure before the war, became plain during the conflict. "This is essentially a people's contest," he wrote. "On the side of the Union, it is a struggle for maintaining in the world, that form, and substance of government, whose main object is, to elevate the condition of men—to lift artificial weights from all shoulders—to clear the paths of laudable pursuit for all—to afford all, an unfettered start, and a fair chance, in the race of life. . . . I am most happy to believe that the plain people understand, and appreciate this." At an earlier period, and on various occasions, he declared that equality of rights and privileges was the central intent of democracy. As he put it during the discussion of the Kansas-Nebraska Act: "No man is good enough to govern another man without that man's consent." And he once gave the idea a still more emphatic statement: "As I would not be a *slave,* so I would not be a *master.* This expresses my idea of democracy. Whatever differs from this, to the extent of the difference, is no democracy."

The perils to democracy, in his view, were numerous. One was materialism, or selfish wealth, or what he called Mammon. "The plainest print," he said in 1857, after the Dred Scott decision, "cannot be read through a gold eagle." Another, to which he often adverted, was demagogy. He spoke scornfully of the troublemaking politicians who were more anxious to serve error than truth; that is, demagogues. These demagogues, he said, were enemies of the whole people: they "are subtle, and profound, on the rights of minorities. They are not partial to that power which made the Constitution, and speaks from the preamble, calling itself, 'We, the People.'" They were adroit in corrupting the electorate. The plotters of secession, for example, "commenced by an insidious drugging of the public mind. They invented an ingenious sophism, which, if conceded, was followed by perfectly logical steps, through all its incidents, to the complete destruction of the Union. This sophism is that any State of the Union may . . . lawfully and peacefully withdraw from the Union. . . ." The word *politician,* in Lincoln's vocabulary, usually had an unfavorable connotation.

As for the success of democracy, Lincoln was sure that this was two-thirds proved. He said this in almost so many words. "Our popular government," he wrote, "has often been called an experiment. Two points in it, our people have already settled—the successful *establishing,* and the successful *administering,* of it. One still remains—its successful *maintenance* against a formidable attempt to overthrow it." The question of maintenance did not concern the nation alone; it concerned the world. "And this issue," he declared, "embraces more than the fate of these United States. It presents to the whole family of man, the question, whether a constitutional republic, or a democracy—a government of the people, by the same people—can, or cannot, maintain its territorial integrity against its own domestic foes. . . . It forces us to ask: 'Is there, in all republics, this inherent, and fatal weakness?' " But he was confident of the outcome. When the war had endured three years, he told the Sanitary Fair in Philadelphia: "For the American people, so far as my knowledge enables me to speak, I say we are going through on this line if it takes three years more."

Lincoln thus gave something more than the two cheers for democracy that the novelist E. M. Forster has given it; say, two and a half cheers. Superior as it was to any other form of government, when bad men—politicians, demagogues—obtained an ascendancy, it worked badly. That is, it worked badly when deflected by an Aaron Burr, a James Buchanan, or a Vallandigham. It worked well when leadership was exercised by honest, sagacious men. Aberrations from the true path, however, would probably be brief, for the majority of the people would not be fooled very long. Lincoln would have applied to American democracy the apologue he once related of himself. "For such an awkward fellow," he said, "I am pretty sure-footed. . . . I remember the evening of the day in 1858 that decided the contest for the Senate between Mr. Douglas and myself . . . dark, rainy, and gloomy. I had been reading the returns, and had ascertained that we had lost the legislature, and started to go home. The path had been worn hogbacked and was slippery. Both my feet slipped from under me, but I recovered myself and lit clear; and I said to myself, 'It is a slip and not a fall.' " The American democracy was awkward but sure-footed; it experienced some bad slips, but it did not fall.

Thus repeating Lincoln's few formal statements upon democracy, or government by the whole people, we must confess that they do not carry us far into the subject. They would not have impressed Tocqueville or John Stuart Mill. They left Lincoln in Charles Camp's category of Americans who lived in the rich experience of democracy without analyzing its underlying theories. If we summarize his tenets under a half-dozen heads, as we can, this will perhaps make clearer both their values and their limitations:

Men may believe fervently in liberty but reject democracy. Lincoln's position was a pole apart from that of such thinkers as Burke, a passionate libertarian but no democrat. Burke wrote that he never addressed himself to the vulgar, nor to that which alone governs the vulgar, their passions. Lincoln pointedly addressed himself to the vulgar —the plain people—and to their reason.

Lincoln believed in a government by the whole people, without material restrictions. He did not share John Adams' opinion that a governing class was needed—an elite qualified by special mental and moral fitness. Neither did he share John Stuart Mill's fear of the tyranny of the majority, which led Mill to insist on special safeguards for minority rights, and finally made him a pioneer in the movement for proportional representation. Lincoln's faith in the whole people came near being absolute.

He believed emphatically in the egalitarian principle, telling the 164th Ohio in August 1864, that "every man has a right to be equal to every other man." But he believed with still greater emphasis that our society must be an *open* society, its members given full opportunity to apply their talents without hindrance and to rise to the height of their powers. Everyone should have "an open field and a fair chance." I am the temporary occupant of the White House, he told another Ohio regiment; and "I am a living witness that any one of your children may look to come here as my father's child has."

His pragmatic view of democracy was shaped largely by his special environment of the agricultural Middle West, where men were shrewd, well informed, full of common-sense sagacity, tinctured with idealism, and sufficiently homogeneous to be good-natured and tolerant. Had he seen more of the kind of population already filling much of the Eastern cities, he would possibly have shared Mill's fear that the stable agrarian elements in the democracy might not be strong enough to balance the more volatile urban and industrial elements. Had he seen the face of industrialism more clearly, he might have worried more.

He realized perfectly that the quality of democracy depends heavily on the quality of leadership. This was the exact converse of Senator Ratcliffe's theory that it is hopeless to do much about leadership until we improve the masses. Lincoln's position that democracy works admirably under a Washington or Jefferson, and fails to work under the Pierces and Buchanans, is not only borne out by history, but is supported by the instinctive feeling of the people. A democracy thirsts for nothing more than sagacious leadership, and is never so happy as when it appears.

In exercising leadership, Lincoln—as both his words and deeds show—always remained practical. He placed a heavy reliance on argument and logic; on the come-let-us-reason-together spirit. He used calm, dispassionate exposition. But he also used the practical tools of the politics of his day—patronage, pressure, conferences with legislative leaders which involved astute bargaining, and once or twice, such dubious steps as those he took to make sure that the House would pass the Thirteenth Amendment.

Springing from and guiding an optimistic people, he was always an optimist about democracy. He would have been the last man to sell America short.

The most remarkable of the features of his thought here enumerated is his optimism, for seldom if ever has American democracy offered more repulsive aspects than between 1830 and 1860. He believed in its virtues; but did they really outweigh its vices? Governor Thomas Ford, whom Lincoln knew, wrote a history of Illinois portraying the political life of the prairie state in lurid hues. He flayed his predecessors in the State House with merciless scalpel; he showed how petty were the men who governed Illinois in Lincoln's youth, how mean their motives, how sordid their acts. The Illinoisans of that generation cruelly maltreated Black Hawk and his Sac and Fox Indians; they brutally murdered Joseph Smith and his brother, and forced the Mormons at musket-point across the Mississippi. They indulged in wild extravagance during the internal improvements era, and wavered on the brink of debt repudiation later. The looser side of political morals was illustrated by the conduct of Governor Joel A. Matteson who, after almost gaining the Senate seat which Lincoln wanted, was proved guilty of theft from the state treasury, and compelled to restore to it nearly a quarter of a million dollars. The Alton riots and the murder of Elijah Lovejoy, the abolitionist martyr, placed a sad blot on the shield of Illinois.

On the national scene political democracy had even more dismaying aspects. From Lincoln's point of view the Mexican War was impossible to defend. The quarrel over slavery had undermined the political integrity of the country, and a succession of presidential defectives—the commonplace Fillmore, the forcible-feeble Pierce, the timid Buchanan—offered no policy to meet the mounting crisis but evasion and postponement. Violence stained all political life. The House of Representatives, said Thaddeus Stevens, when he entered it in 1849 was a place of bowie knives, revolvers, and howling demons. What a lurid light was thrown on the workings of democracy by bleeding Kansas; by the assault of Brooks upon Sumner in the Capitol itself; by the eclipse of civil liberties throughout the South; and by the ideas of territorial grabbing embodied in the Ostend Manifesto, and the filibustering raids on Cuba and Central America. The nation's descent into civil war was by a series of episodes that indicted democracy, and the conflict itself seemed to mark its breakdown. *Punch* published a cartoon which presented the shade of George III poking the shade of George Washington in the ribs and ejaculating: "What d'ye think of your fine republic now? Eh? Eh?"

Lincoln had an ample firsthand experience of democracy in its demagogic, reckless phases. As a young legislator he had played his part in the internal improvement craze which fastened a load of debt on his young state; he had been one of the Sangamon delegation whose adroit lobbying removed the capital from Vandalia to Springfield. He saw realistically the vicious features of spoils-system government in the Jacksonian era. The Democratic Party had blindly followed Old Hickory wherever he led it; or, as Lincoln put it, the hungry Democratic ticks had stuck to the tail of the Hermitage lion till his death. He thought the acts of the proslavery administrations just before the war disgraceful. "Our Republican robe," he said in the Peoria speech of 1854, "is soiled and trailed in the dust."

Lincoln in his wartime dealings with democracy experienced three painful failures. His passionate desire during his first month in office was to avert war, an end toward which he strove at any cost save the sacrifice of principle; but his labors were thwarted when passionate Southerners fired on Fort Sumter. His principal effort in the next seventeen months, second only to the prosecution of the war, was to persuade the border states to accept a plan of gradual compensated emancipation, joined with a program for colonizing the freedmen abroad. He put the utmost intensity of feeling into this effort. "Oh," he said to Isaac Arnold and Owen Lovejoy on July 13, 1862, "how I wish the border States would accept my proposition. Then you, Lovejoy, and you, Arnold, and all of us, would not have lived in vain!" He thought acceptance of his plan would soon lead to the end of the conflict; but Maryland and Delaware, Kentucky and Missouri, rejected it. In the next eighteen months, as the war dragged to its close, he signally failed to persuade the majority in Congress to adopt a moderate scheme of reconstruction; and in 1864 he had to veto the vindictive scheme embodied in the Wade-Davis bill. His own Cabinet so often opposed him that he said he hoped he would have more influence with the next administration. The policies on which he most set his heart, in short, broke down. Meanwhile, he might well have complained of public impatience, of the popular refusal to keep the armies sufficiently filled to avert a draft, of the widespread profiteering and cheating, and of such Congressional mischief as the attempt to dictate a new Cabinet just after Fredericksburg.

He never complained, and never lost faith. Why was it that during all his discouragements, amid all the demagogy, knavery, and selfishness of the time, he maintained an unyielding belief in the superior virtues of democracy? His best-trusted associate, Secretary Seward, sometimes lost faith in the people. We who bear the responsibility in Washington, Seward wrote his wife in 1862, see the war as a sad, painful, fearful reality. "To the public, who are not directly engaged in it, it is a novel, a play. . . . They weary and grow restive if the action of the war drags, or loses its intensity. They pronounce the piece a failure, and propose to drive the manager out of the theatre. Who could believe that nations could be made or saved in civil war, when the people act like this?" On another occasion Seward wrote that nothing preserved his sense of philosophy about the American democracy but reading history. "Selfishness crops out in everything, everywhere. It offends and alarms us constantly; but we learn from history that selfishness always existed. . . ."

Gideon Welles likewise lost faith. After watching the unprincipled antics of the defeatist Congressman Fernando Wood, he burst out: "But the whole city of New York is alike leprous and rotten." In such vicious communities, he thought, free suffrage was dangerous, and some outside control imperatively needed. During his youth Welles had believed that the popular voice was right; "but alas," he wrote, "experience has shaken the confidence I once had." In short, he doubted that democracy could succeed among what he termed "the strange materials that compose a majority of the population in our large cities." Thaddeus

Stevens came to feel a yet deeper distrust. He was called the Great Commoner, and he was supposed to cherish a passionate attachment to democracy. Yet during the war and Reconstruction he came to a sardonic belief that misgovernment was chronic, and when near his death he commented: "With all this great struggle of years in Washington, and the fearful sacrifice of life and treasure, I see little hope for the republic."

An impulsive but equally caustic and pessimistic statement was expressed by William Tecumseh Sherman when he entered the war in the summer of 1861. He wrote home that he was in command of six regiments of volunteers called by courtesy soldiers, and that God alone could foresee the issue. He went on: "Our adversaries have the weakness of slavery in their midst to offset our democracy, and 'tis beyond human wisdom to say which is the greater evil." During his residence in Mississippi, Sherman had apparently been infected by the scorn which such Southern leaders as Robert Toombs, Howell Cobb, and Judah P. Benjamin always expressed for democracy. When Alexander H. Stephens, defending the Union before the Georgia legislature in 1860, asked what form of government could be preferred to America's, Toombs exclaimed "England's" —and England still had an aristocratic government.

A few years more, and during the Reconstruction period the voice of disillusionment filled the land. Henry Adams saw little hope for democracy. Ambrose Bierce, an Indianan sprung from the plain people, decided that popular government was a vast fraud. In *The Devil's Dictionary* he stated his conclusions: "Politics: The conduct of public affairs for private advantage." "Deliberation: The act of examining one's bread to see which side it is buttered on." Mark Twain was mordantly cynical about democracy in his novel *The Gilded Age,* and one of his paragraphs on the free, bold, egalitarian West in *Life on the Mississippi* was hardly a paean to its virtues. He wrote:

How solemn and beautiful is the thought that the earliest pioneer of civilization . . . is never the steamboat, never the railroad, never the newspapers, never the Sabbath School, never the missionary—but always whisky! Such is the case. Look history over; you will see. The missionary comes after the whisky—I mean, he arrives after the whisky has arrived; next comes the poor immigrant with axe and hoe and rifle; next, the trader; next the miscellaneous rush; next the gambler, the desperado, the highwayman, and all their kindred in sin of both sexes; and next, the smart chap who has bought up an old grant that covered all the lands; this brings in the lawyer tribe; the vigilance committee brings the undertaker. All these interests bring the newspaper; the newspaper starts up politics and a railroad; all hands turn to and build a church and a jail—and behold, civilization is established forever in the land.

To comprehend why Lincoln felt none of this cynicism, none of this disillusionment, we would look in vain in his writings. He often voiced his faith in democracy, but never gave explicit reasons—probably because he thought them unnecessary. And yet it is not true to say that he simply took democracy on intuitive faith. His policies, his acts, show that he had certain large bases for his confidence in its workings.

He founded this confidence largely upon what he saw of the people about him in the first fifty years of his life. That the inhabitants of the Old Northwest, from Ohio to Iowa, were then a folk of superior character and intelligence, is a fact attested by many observers. The second generation in that fertile area read the New York *Weekly Tribune,* founded colleges, and molded new communities with the tough idealism depicted by Herbert Quick and Hamlin Garland. Good studies of this society, founded on firsthand observation, may be found in Edward Eggleston's novel of Lincoln's younger days in Illinois, *The Graysons,*

Clark E. Carr's picture of Galesburg entitled *The Illini*, and the letters of such leaders as Edward Beecher of Jacksonville and Josiah B. Grinnell of the Iowa town he named. Carl Schurz in epistle after epistle to German friends expatiated on Western intelligence, energy, and liberalism. Just after the election of 1856 he wrote from Wisconsin:

> The last weeks were times when public matters made more demands than ordinarily upon the American system. You over there in your decrepit Europe can hardly imagine how a great idea can stir up the masses of the people to their depths, and how an enthusiastic struggle for principles can thrust aside for a certain time all other interests, even the materialistic ones. . . . A general struggle of opinions among a free people has in it something unbelievably imposing; and you never see with greater clearness what a far-reaching influence political freedom exercises upon the development of the masses.

Richard Cobden, the great English liberal, made an equally emphatic statement after he toured the Northwest in 1859. Impressed by the high level of decorum, education, and interest in public affairs, he wrote home that his confidence in popular government had been quickened. "The concentrated earnestness," he remarked, "with which political parties were at work in the United States, inspired me with a full faith that the people of the country would, in spite of the difficulties and dangers of their political issues, work out their salvation." This earnestness likewise heartened Lincoln. He himself transcended the virtues of his time and section; as Herbert Croly later put it, he was more than an American. He was thoughtful where the frontier was thoughtless, studious where it was ignorant, magnanimous where it was vindictive. Still, he saw that the average was high. He founded his belief in democracy on the same rock as Whitman's, a sympathetic appreciation of the virtues of the common man.

This rock was fortified by a special set of principles expressed in the two basic American documents, the Declaration of Independence and the Constitution. Another reason for Lincoln's confidence was his belief that the spirit of these two documents had permeated the democratic mass. For both he felt a strong reverence. Of the Constitution he said in Congress in 1848 that it should not lightly be touched: "It can scarcely be made better than it is." For the Declaration he expressed a still deeper attachment, and whenever its spirit warred with the letter of the Constitution, he stood by its spirit. Every nation, he said in Chicago in 1856, needs a central idea. "The central idea in our political public opinion was, and until recently continued to be, the equality of man"—the idea of the Declaration. This was more than a purely national idea, however; it could and should be made world-wide in potency. Out of the Revolution, he told the New Jersey Senate in Trenton in 1860, had come something larger than American independence—"that something that held out a great promise to all the people of the world to all time to come." Faith in the American idea, faith in the American world mission—these two beliefs, Lincoln felt, had given our democracy a pervasive inspiration.

His confidence in the people, confidence in the inspiring charters the fathers of the nation had given them, and confidence in the world future of their central idea, he all summed up in a few sentences of his appeal to the Border State Representatives in July 1862. "You are patriots and statesmen," he said. "Consider this proposition, and at the least commend it to the consideration of your States and people." He went on:

"As you would perpetuate popular government for the best people in the world, I beseech that you do in no wise omit this. Our common country is in great peril demanding the loftiest views and boldest action to bring it speedy relief. Once relieved, its form of government is saved to the world, its beloved history and cherished memories are vindicated, and its happy future fully assured and rendered inconceivably grand."

For all his faith and optimism, Lincoln did not expect too much of democracy, because he had a correct idea of its true nature. The men who grew cynical about it like Sherman, or discouraged like Thad Stevens, thought of it as an achieved state of political society, a goal, a terminal situation; hence its defects seemed to them horrible. Lincoln knew it was nothing of the sort. Democracy is a process, an unending struggle, a hard, grueling battle. Its best benefits are not the easy garlands found on arrival at a superior political position; they are the toughness, the heroic constancy, the stamina, developed during the desperate climb upward. Democracy is not a serene attainment; it is an incessant effort, marked by ignominious falls, heartbreaking defeats, and almost intolerable trials. Lincoln almost said this in so many words, telling some troops to gird themselves for the heavy postwar work ahead: "When you return to your homes rise up to the height of a generation of men worthy of a free Government." He said it in effect again and again. His writings cheered Americans on to the struggle and the sacrifice. He would have endorsed the crisp statement by Carl Schurz, who declared that the revolutionary idealists of Europe might be startled by the seamy side of American affairs. They would see:

the most contradictory tendencies and antagonistic movements openly at work, side by side, or against one another, enlightenment and stupid bigotry, good citizenship and lawlessness, benevolent and open-handed public spirit and rapacious greed, democracy and slavery, independent spirit and subservience to party despotism and to predominant public opinion—all this in bewildering confusion. The newly arrived European democrat . . . without having had any practical experience of a democracy at work, beholding it for the first time, asks himself: "Is this really a people living in freedom? Is this the realization of my ideal?"

But, Schurz went on, democracy is essentially a struggle. The acute observer would soon see this:

> He is puzzled and perplexed until it dawns on him that, in a condition of real freedom, man manifests himself, not as he ought to be, but as he is, with all his bad as well as his good qualities, instincts, and impulses; with all his attributes of strength as well as all his weaknesses; that this, therefore, is not an ideal state, but simply a state in which the forces of good have a free field as against the forces of evil, and in which the victories of virtue, of enlightenment, and of progress are not achieved by some power or agency outside of the people, for their benefit, but *by* the people themselves.

> Such victories of the forces of good may be slow in being accomplished, but they will be all the more thorough and durable in their effects, because they will be the product of the people's own thought and effort.

Seeing democracy as an incessant contest, a never-ending battle, Lincoln's faith in it was buoyed by his sense that while it was going hard, it was also going well. He had an increasing conviction from 1848 onward that the masses were being possessed by a stern moral conviction that would ultimately regenerate the country. They were rising to meet the demands of a cause larger than any they had known since 1789. Other men understood this ocean-heave of democratic idealism. William Cullen Bryant was one. When the presidential campaign of 1856 closed with a Republican vote for Frémont of 1,341,264 against 1,838,169 for Buchanan, Bryant was exultant. The party of freedom had swept New England, carried New York,

Ohio, Wisconsin, and Michigan, and made great gains in Illinois and Indiana. Public opinion in these states, wrote Bryant, had shifted from indecision to resolution. "If we look back to 1848, when we conducted a Presidential election on this very ground of opposition to the spread of slavery, we shall see that we have made immense strides. . . . We were then comparatively weak, we are now strong; we then counted our thousands, we now count our millions; we could then point to our respectable minorities in a few States, we now point to State after State. . . . The cause is not going back—it is going rapidly forward; the freesoil party of 1848 is the nucleus of the Republican Party of 1856; but with what accessions of numbers, of moral power, of influence, not merely in public assemblies, but at the domestic fireside!"

Lincoln had felt the pulse of the great movement begin to beat with new energy when the Wilmot Proviso almost passed Congress. He felt the movement grow in urgency and strength as Mrs. Stowe published *Uncle Tom's Cabin,* as the Underground Railroad gave defiance to the Fugitive Slave Act, as millions of Northerners rose in wrath against what they deemed Douglas' betrayal of freedom in the Kansas-Nebraska Act, and as the Republican Party became a giant of crusading idealism. The North was presenting the impressive spectacle which gave the French liberal, Elie Gasparin, his title for the book he published early in the war, *The Uprising of a Great People.*

The war brought the upheaval to its climax. It did not astonish Lincoln to find that depressing as were the confusion, cowardice, and meanness revealed by the conflict, far outweighing these defects were the displays of heroism, devotion, and generosity.

The plain people rose to save the Union and vindicate the type of government which would elevate the condition of all men. Countless soldiers proved ready to give the last full measure of devotion. Countless mothers were proud to lay their costliest sacrifice on the national altar. Proud,

in fact, was the word used by the mother of Robert Gould
Shaw when she was told that Governor John A. Andrew
had given her son the command of the famous new Negro
regiment, the Fifty-fourth Massachusetts. She said, "I am
nearly as proud as I would be to hear that he had been
shot." Later she heard that also.

Countless fathers showed the spirit of Commodore
Smith, who, said Hawthorne, uttered the finest short speech
of the war. His son Jo commanded the frigate *Congress* in
Hampton Roads when the Merrimac began battering her
to pieces, and the old commodore knew that his boy would
die before he hauled down the colors. When informed that
the *Congress* had struck its banner he therefore said, with
simple feeling, "Then Jo's dead"—and Jo *was* dead. He
died before the flag came down.

There were countless public officers as devoted as the
two Assistant Secretaries in the War Department who
literally worked themselves to death; or as the much-tried
Stanton himself, whom an aide once surprised with his
head bowed on his desk, weeping and exclaiming over and
over, "God help me to do my duty! God help me to do
my duty!" These men and women were exponents of democracy as a never-ending process, a contest, an ordeal,
toughening them by trials and defeats more often than it
exhilarated them by victories. Lincoln knew that, as Schurz
put it, democracy was not an ideal state, but an arena in
which good had a free field against evil, and in which the
people were made great by the fact that they achieved progress not as the gift of some outside agency, but by their
own hard struggle.

One historian, unlike Henry Adams' Mr. Gore, knew
what democracy was and what it could accomplish. When
the war closed John Lothrop Motley wrote from Austria to
tell a Boston friend how glad he was that the nightmare of
blood and fire had ended. "Believing in no government but
that of the people, respecting no institutions but democratic
institutions," he declared, "I feel sure that the future of the

whole world is in our hands if we are true to ourselves." He paid tribute to Grant as a master of the art of war—"What could be more heroic than his stupendous bashfulness?" Of Lincoln he wrote that he was reluctant to speak for fear of overenthusiasm. "But I am sure that through all future ages, there will be a halo around that swarthy face, and a glory about that long, lean, uncouth figure such as history only accords to its saints and sages." Lincoln would have shrunk from this as overenthusiasm indeed.

But the president would heartily have endorsed the statement which Motley sent at the same time to Thomas Hughes, the author of *Tom Brown's School Days*. "My dear Hughes," he wrote, "the true hero of the whole war—the one I respect and admire even beyond Lincoln and Grant . . . is the American people."

Chapter 6

Lincoln as More Than a Statesman

1

IT HAS LONG BEEN THE FASHION for popular writers and speakers to view Lincoln romantically, not realistically. Yet for regarding him realistically, without attempt to magnify or depreciate, we have this warrant, that he was himself a stern realist. He was a realist about his associates, Chase, Seward, Stanton, McClellan. He was a realist about himself and his limitations. "Money!" he exclaimed when somebody wanted to discuss war finances. "I don't know anything about money. I never had enough of my own to fret me, and I have no opinion about it in any way." He was a realist about the sweeping forces of the time, saying bluntly that he had not controlled events, but events had controlled him. He was a realist about the springs of public support, remarking sagely in one crisis: "I do not need sympathy nearly so much as I need success." He was a realist in always placing great objects above small ones. When the politicians protested against putting a new draft into effect in the midst of the presidential campaign of 1864, because it might cost him the election, he demanded:

"What is the presidency worth to me if I have no country?"

Lincoln would have been quick to say that the effort to paint any man as ideal is absurd, and the first to dissent from many of the adulatory judgments of Nicolay and Hay.

The tendency to soften the lineaments of this strange, quaint, rugged, and powerful man has been natural, for his heart was as great as his brain; but it does injustice to his most important public aspect, his tough, forcible, hard-hitting side. Too much has been said of his kindness, mildness, and magnanimity. These traits were real, but so also were his calculating shrewdness, his firmness, his occasional harshness, and his infrequent but unforgettable bursts of anger. He said "no" with a good-natured air, but he said it often and positively. In dealing with cunning politicians he had a cunning of his own that Stanton called genius. He pardoned sleeping sentries and deserters not merely because he was kindly, but because he had a keen instinct for policy; he was no worshiper of generals, he disliked military despotism, he saw that the North had to depend on masses of volunteers, and he knew that if the regular army officers imposed the death penalty without check, volunteering would stop.

Not often, but more than once, he exhibited an ebullition of anger like Washington's at Monmouth. Donn Piatt, temporary commander in Baltimore, once gave General William Birney what Lincoln thought quite premature and damaging orders to recruit men for a Negro brigade. Piatt tells of the penalty he paid:

Then came a curt summons, ordering me to appear at the War Department. I obeyed . . . Being informed that the Secretary was at the Executive Mansion, I repaired there, sent in my card, and was at once shown into the presence, not of Mr. Stanton but of the President. I do not care to recall the words of Mr. Lincoln. I wrote them out that night, for I was threatened with a shameful dismissal from the service, and I intended appealing to the public. They were exceedingly severe, for the President was in a rage. I was not allowed to say a word in my own defence, and was only permitted to say that I would countermand the order as well as I could. I was saved cashiering through the influence of Stanton and Chase . . .

Another misapprehension is all too common. Lincoln was not a giant surrounded by dwarfs, and moving as a free agent, with the other personages of the crowded drama subordinate to his intellect and vision. Such a conception is subject to correction on two counts.

To begin with, if Lincoln was unquestionably the greatest of the Northern leaders in the Civil War, he was nevertheless but the strongest of a group of great-statured men. The hardest work of dealing with the upheaval fell, under Lincoln, to three lawyers drawn from the area between the Mohawk and Maumee Rivers: Seward, Stanton, and Chase. Each, like Lincoln, was (as we have noted) totally inexperienced in his new field; each carried forward his work with blunders aplenty, but with pluck, energy, and growing skill; each refused to let it be obstructed or defeated; and each so exhausted himself that he emerged from the war with shattered health, and soon died—Stanton in four years, Seward in seven, and Chase in eight. Let us not underrate this powerful trio. And, in the second place, Lincoln had to act within a tremendous stream of forces, the chief of which were a Congress always headstrong and independent, and a public opinion of decidedly greater variety, turbulence, and force than that of the South—which is saying much. This Congress and public opinion had to be consulted at every turn.

In its more routine aspects, the special quality of Lincoln's statesmanship was its extraordinary realism or practicality. In his month-to-month work, what set him apart from Seward, Stanton, and Chase and above preceding or succeeding Presidents was his grasp of what was practicable at any given moment. He would never have reached national leadership but for this unerring instinct. Seward in the 1850's had rashly gone too far; he had uttered sentiments in his "higher law" speech and again in his "irrepressible conflict" speech which struck most citizens as excessively radical—and he failed of the prize. He forgot the truth expressed in Greville's maxim, "Only the Tories can carry Liberal Measures"—that is, only the man who is trusted can carry even the soundest measures if they originate with distrusted men. Edward Bates, in contrast, had not gone far enough in the 1850's; he had seemed lukewarm on the slavery question, and he too failed of the prize.

Lincoln had gone just far enough. He had been resolute on the two great principles of the wrongfulness of slavery, and the necessity of excluding it from the Territories; but he had stopped at that point. He had not risked offending cautious men by declaring what further steps he would take to put slavery, after its containment, in the way of ultimate extinction. That he left to time and the fit occasion. Throughout the Civil War he had a far surer sense than other men of the degrees by which revolutionary measures could be effected, and of the times for putting them into effect.

As his secretaries John Hay and John G. Nicolay put it, he was a great opportunist, in the good sense of the word, before the term opportunism was invented; in modern parlance, he was blessed with an uncanny sense of timing. He was, as Walter Bagehot said of Sir Robert Peel, the uncommon man of common opinions.

In his day-to-day work this realistic sense for the occasion, as the French call it, combined with his practical acumen in the leadership of men, much more than offset his manifest weaknesses as an executive. He was by no means distinguished as an administrator. Entering the White House without the slightest administrative training, his haphazard, unsystematic, unbusinesslike ways were the despair of secretaries and bureaucrats. His biographer John T. Morse correctly declares that "he had no capacity for business." His laxities were the theme of bitter complaint by the admiring Gideon Welles.

Salmon P. Chase declared midway in the war that there was no Administration in the proper sense of the word—that is, no coordination of the executive departments; and he wrote a friend in 1863 that when he wanted to know what was going on outside the Treasury, he had to send a boy out for a copy of the New York *Herald*. Lincoln gave close attention to the work of two departments, State and War, but with the others he seldom meddled, and his Administration was rather a loose coalition than a unitary body. He had no such capacity as Woodrow Wilson showed fifty-five years later in mobilizing the economic energies of the land. Their dispersed, unorganized character would have made the task extremely difficult, but we have no record of his interest in enlisting businessmen and industrialists, and we may well wonder why the list of those employed—Thomas A. Scott, Peter H. Watson, the youthful Andrew Carnegie, Herman Haupt, and a few others—was not far longer.

Repeatedly, as was inevitable, he committed grave errors of judgment. Thomas M. Clarke, Episcopal Bishop of Rhode Island, called on him in late June, 1861, to find him just completing his message to the special session opening on July 4. "The result of this war is a question of resources," said the President. "That side will win in the end where the money holds out longest; but if the war should continue until it costs us *five hundred millions of dollars*" (dwelling on this sum with emphasis, as if it were the largest amount conceivable) "the resources of the country are such that the credit of the Government will be better than it was at the close of the Revolution." Yet in the end a sum much nearer five thousand millions was required. Like others North and South, Lincoln thought the war would be short when it should have been plain it would be long. Too little and too late must be our verdict on various measures of 1861 and 1862.

In dealing with military affairs his general conception was quite sound. Thus he wrote Don Carlos Buell early in the war a correct statement of the problem. "I state my own idea of this war to be," he declared, "that we have the greater numbers, and the enemy have the greater facility of concentrating forces upon points of collision; that we must fail unless we have some way of making our advantage an overmatch for his; and that this can only be done by menacing him with superior forces at different points at the same time . . ." In other words, the North must make the most of its superior numbers, and must minimize the Southern advantage of inside lines.

Lincoln is not to be blamed because in a few instances public opinion took a military decision out of his hands. After Bull Run, General Winfield Scott burst out: "I am the greatest coward in America. I have fought this battle, sir, against my judgment; I think the President of the United States ought to remove me today for doing it." In this statement lay an implied rebuke to Lincoln and his associates. Scott had advised against an offensive thrust into Virginia in July, 1861, on military grounds; Lincoln and his Cabinet had overruled Scott on political grounds, declaring that the public would brook no further delay. The event had proved Scott right, but the real culprit was the public which had responded so excitably to the cry of "On to Richmond!" Nor could Lincoln be blamed because one commander after another, McClellan, Pope, Burnside, Meade, fell short of what was expected of him.

But he could be censured for some very unhappy interferences with military strategy. What, for example, of his division of the command in western Virginia in 1862 among Frémont, Banks, and McDowell? More distinctly, perhaps, he can be censured, as General Sir Frederick Maurice shows, for not finding a means of conveying his entirely sound ideas of general policy, and his clear grasp of political necessities, to his earlier generals. The failure of Lincoln and McClellan to understand each other may have been mainly the fault of McClellan, but it was partly the fault of Lincoln; and when in 1864 a complete understanding was reached with the commander, Lincoln knowing how to give advice and support to Grant, and Grant knowing how to give information to Lincoln, the highroad to victory was open.

2

Yet in the field of practical statesmanship these shortcomings, and still others which we could easily define, were far more than counterbalanced by Lincoln's supreme dexterity in managing both his associates and the mass opinion of the country. At first hesitant, he quickly became a true leader, relying more and more on his own judgment as he found that it was better than Seward's, Blair's, McClellan's, or Halleck's. Before long, in Gideon Welles's phrase, he had developed "wonderful self-reliance." He became the indispensable man of the crisis. "He could have dispensed with any one of his cabinet," writes Welles, "and the administration [would] not have been impaired, but it would have been difficult if not impossible to have selected anyone who could have filled the office of chief magistrate as successfully as Mr. Lincoln." Above all, he was never too far ahead of the plain people and never once behind them. A revealing document is the voluminous diary kept during the war by George Templeton Strong, a Wall Street lawyer of aristocratic connections and intellectual tastes. He saw much of Lincoln, and as treasurer of the Sanitary Commission repeatedly talked with him. At the outset, he was distrustful of the man; Lincoln seemed untutored, inexperienced, and inadequate. As the conflict continued, however, Strong's admiration increased. At the end, under date of May 14, 1865, we find him writing of a friend,

General Martin T. McMahon, who had accompanied Lincoln's funeral train westward:

> He says nothing in all this unprecedented manifestation of public mourning has impressed him so much as the sight that was frequent along the line of the railroad of some solitary husbandman laying down his spade or hoe or stopping his team half a mile away, taking off his hat, and remaining uncovered while the train passed by and as long as it was in sight. No prince, no leader of a people, was ever so lamented as this unpolished Western lawyer was and is. His name is Faithful and True. He will stand in history beside Washington, perhaps higher.

The terrible difficulty of this task of controlling public opinion, which meant swaying Congress and the elections of 1862 and 1864, is not easily grasped. We must remember the complete failure of Madison to preserve a decent national unity in the War of 1812, and the partial failure of Polk in the Mexican War, both acting under conditions far simpler. The war was a political war, that is, dominated by political factors. In a conflict with a foreign power national unity is seldom so difficult to attain as in an intestinal war, where large factions almost always sympathize with those in revolt. Yet without a fair degree of political unity in 1861-1865, the government would break down; without popular zeal to furnish volunteers and popular resolution to endure a draft, the armies would melt away; without general willingness to pay cruel taxes, the national effort would sink in ruin. The war, so far as possible, had to be a war of the whole people. It could not be a Republican war, but must embrace all loyal Democrats. Still less could it be a war by and for Radical Republicans, as Chase, Sumner, and Wade desired, or by and for conservative Republicans, as Seward sometimes seemed to wish. The moment Lincoln seemed to give the war effort a partisan or factional direction, he and the country were lost.

It was therefore proper that a preponderance of Lincoln's thinking and toils should be bent toward the attainment and preservation of harmony. When Oliver P. Morton, a former Democrat who became the able war governor of Indiana, complained of arms shortages, Lincoln returned a patient explanation that the country did not have munitions enough for all; that it must share them around; that the points of greatest danger needed them most; and that Indiana was far safer than Washington, where he sat within sound of the cannon of a hostile army of one hundred thousand men. "I am compelled to watch all points," he said. All points indeed! He became the grand harmonizer of the North. He had to deal with Congress, where factions snarled at each other and the Radicals set up their Committee on the Conduct of the War to snap at his heels. He had to deal with impatient New Englanders, reluctant border-State men, selfish business interests, venomous New York and Ohio Copperheads, and a dozen other elements. Once, in the summer of 1864, beset by the McClellan Democrats on one side and the Frémont Radicals on the other, he almost despaired, but even that crisis he surmounted.

Any reader of Lincoln's wartime letters must be struck by one fact: the extent to which they are addressed, not to his friends, but to his opponents and critics. All readers must be struck by another characteristic: the refusal in these letters to assert that he had been right, or his critics wrong, or in any way to address himself to posterity. After the election of 1864 he explicitly said that he would not take the victory as personal; that it "is no pleasure to me to triumph over anyone"; and that "so long as I have been here, I have not willingly planted a thorn in any man's bosom." After Appomattox he told an audience that all credit went to the army; "no part of the honor, for plan or execution, is mine." Readers of the letters must also note that, while not neglecting appeals to the sympathy, the pride, and even the fears of recipients, they emphasized cool persuasion and objective argument. As Nicolay and Hay write: "To still the quarrels of factions, to allay the jealousies of statesmen, to compose the rivalries of generals, to soothe the vanity of officials, to prompt the laggard, to curb the ardent, to sustain the faltering, was a substratum of daily routine underlying the great events of campaigns, battles, and high questions of state."

Was it easy? When we see that he never really failed to keep both the masses and the best intelligence of the country with him, we may think it was. But any tendency to believe this is quickly checked by a glance at the course and fortunes of his associates, not one of whom showed a tithe of his skill in solidifying public opinion, and several of whom proved that they were almost wholly out of touch with it.

How completely Seward's famous letter of April 1, 1861, for example, suggesting the propriety of provoking a European war in the hope of thus reuniting the North and South against a common enemy, would have destroyed all public confidence in the Secretary had it been known! Seward owed it to Lincoln's magnanimity and his desire for national unity that the country did not hear of that letter until a generation later, when Nicolay and Hay astounded their readers by publishing it. The elder Charles Francis Adams delivered a Memorial Address on William H. Seward in 1873 in which he made an unhappy attempt to arrogate the chief credit for the merits of the Lincoln Administration to the New Yorker. It fell to the second Charles Francis Adams, in his life of his father, to describe how Seward in his famous Dispatch No. 10, dated May 21, 1861, repeated the blunder of April 1, and how this bellicose paper, which Lincoln first drastically toned down, and then earmarked to be held confidential and secret in the London legation, was entirely misconceived by the minister to England. Adams thought it had been dictated by an impetuous Lincoln!

. . . It puzzled and dismayed Mr. Adams when he first received it. The fiercely aggressive, the well-nigh inconceivable foreign policy it foreshadowed must, he thought, have been forced on the Secretary by the other members of the administration; but, in fact, though Mr. Adams never knew it, that dispatch, in the form in which it was originally drawn up by the Secretary of State and by him submitted to the President, must have been designed to precipitate a foreign war. Moreover, it would inevitably have brought about that result but for Lincoln's unseen intervention.

Seward's impetuosity, if known, would twice have ruined him in the eyes of all sober Northerners. Nor was the accomplished Secretary Chase happier in dealing with Congressional and public opinion. His conduct of the Treasury was in general admirable. He was a man of perfect integrity, great ability, and marked persistence. But he had no powers of persuasion whatever; his relations with Congress show an unbroken record of mutual distrust and bitter wrangling; although he matured a comprehensive scheme for financing the war as early as December, 1861, he could get no Congressional group to support it; and he was totally unable to raise up devoted lieutenants either in politics or in his Treasury work. He knew so little of public sentiment that he entertained the preposterous idea in 1864 that he might supplant Lincoln; and when he resigned that summer he was astonished to find most of the press and other indexes of opinion blithely content to let him go. Montgomery Blair, to take another instance, belonged to a family of highly astute politicians. Yet he committed acts, such as delivering a needless speech on miscegenation, which angered great segments of the public; he was quite unable to get along with other men, denouncing Chase, Seward, and others in violent terms; and after he had assailed Stanton as a "coward and poltroon," his exit from the Cabinet caused much rejoicing and little mourning.

We may compare with the woeful indiscretions of these men, and the story of their failure to gain any wide hold on public affection, the skill with which Lincoln dealt with the most distinctive feature of his Administration, the proclamation of emancipation. The most dangerous subject that any leader could touch, emancipation seemed a three-edged sword, likely to give a mortal wound to any user. First, in the critical border States it affected the property of tens of thousands of the most influential men, and the social interests of nearly all white people. Second, to resort to emancipation meant changing the objects of the war, which had been begun as a struggle to maintain the Union and was now turned into an onslaught against slavery. And third, most Democrats and many conservative Republicans would protest that emancipation was a betrayal of the solemn pledge in the Crittenden resolution which had been voted by an almost unanimous Congress in 1861—a declaration that the war would be fought *only* for the Union.

Yet under the inexorable pressure of events the subject had to be grappled with. Late spring of 1862 found Lincoln, aware that the hour of decision was near, striving to appraise a broad complex of forces and to gauge a crescent change in public feeling. The war had initiated a revolution in Northern thinking upon slavery, and as General Hunter's attempt to free many of the slaves in South Carolina followed that of Frémont to liberate some of them in Missouri, the popular response showed that the torrent of this revolution was carrying great sections of the population with it. As the fighting went on, the masses were saying to themselves: "Slavery is the cause of this horrible contest; it is slavery that is maiming the republic, impoverishing the taxpayer, and filling the land with widows and orphans. We must strike at the roots of our calamity—we must extinguish slavery."

Lincoln, watching the current, had to seize the precise moment for effective action. Mignet, in his history of the French Revolution, remarks: "A man is sometimes a mere feather in an upheaval which carries away the masses; the surge sweeps him along, or leaves him overwhelmed behind; he must keep in advance or be trampled under foot." Despite all Lincoln's reluctance to touch an institution protected by the Constitution, despite his doubts both as to expediency and legal power, he had to keep in mind the truth which Mignet enunciated. It was true that if he moved too soon, conservative men would raise the cry of rash and arbitrary usurpation, and voters would perhaps respond in savage force on election day in 1862. But if he waited too long, majority opinion would follow the Radicals in losing patience with him, and he would be left "overwhelmed behind." He had to understand what the average sentiment of the country would approve, and to mold and guide that sentiment. Simultaneously he had to watch the course of the war, for while he could proclaim emancipation in the moment of victory, he could not do it in the moment of military defeat. He was coming to the rescue of Ethiopia; he must not let it seem that he was calling on Ethiopia to rise and rescue him.

Always a believer in gradualism, Lincoln to the very end of the war thought that gradual emancipation, with compensation to all loyal owners and perhaps all owners loyal or disloyal, would be fairer to the Southern white man, to the Negro, and to the nation as a whole than a sudden destruction of slavery. Be it remembered that he genuinely believed that the Southern masses had been misled by agitators and demagogues. Be it remembered that he was always specially respectful of the border region, where he had been born, and which was represented in his Cabinet by two members, Edward Bates and Montgomery Blair.

He had made repeated appeals to the border States to accept the plan for gradual emancipation, with the aid and cooperation of the general government, which he had persuaded Congress to endorse. On May 19, 1862, he publicly and earnestly besought the border Congressmen to yield to this plan on the ground, among others, that it would shorten the war; for the Southern leaders, if they once saw that Kentucky, Missouri, and Maryland were irretrievably lost, would more readily give up their revolt. And still again, on July 12, calling the border Representatives to the White House, he pleaded with them for acceptance of the scheme. "I assure you," he said, "that, in my opinion, if you had all voted for the resolution in the gradual emancipation message of last March, the war would now be substantially ended." But the border men still resisted his entreaties.

For a variety of reasons the reluctant President could not wait longer; he had to keep at the head of opinion. One reason lay in the fact that the war itself was destroying slavery. Wherever the Union armies penetrated, they abolished servitude, as Lincoln put it, by mere "friction and abrasion." When Port Royal was captured in South Carolina, thousands of Negroes poured into the military camps; and it was partly for this reason that General Hunter issued his much-applauded order of May, 1862, freeing the slaves of South Carolina, Georgia, and Florida wherever they were reached by Northern forces. Lincoln had to revoke that order, but he could not revoke the conditions that elicited it.

As another reason, it was now evident that the war would be long, bloody, and expensive. When McClellan lost his Peninsular campaign, all hope of an early termination of the contest perished. If it were to be long and bloody, emancipation would be justified as a war measure; for it would add to the resources of the North in man power, it would, perhaps, create restlessness among the slaves in certain Southern areas, and, above all, transcending every other consideration, it would put moral purpose into the war. It would give millions of Americans a sense that they were fighting a war of human liberation; it would be hailed in Europe as a Messianic edict, closing an unhappy era in the life of the world's most hopeful nation, and opening a shining new chapter—redeeming the promise of American democracy to the world. Finally, it would meet the more and more exigent demand of Northern opinion, now so steadily crystallizing.

Thus it was that on September 22, 1862, Lincoln devoted the whole strength of the North to the fulfillment of a promise that: "On the first day of January in the year of our Lord one thousand eight hundred and sixty-three, all persons held as slaves within any State or designated part of a State, the people whereof shall then be in rebellion against the United States, shall be then, thenceforward, and forever free." All students of history have agreed that the step was taken at precisely the right moment, and in precisely the right way. It was not taken too soon, or until all decent alternatives had been thoroughly explored. It was assuredly not taken a moment too late.

Much has been written about the limitations of the great proclamation. It did not free the slaves in those areas which had never "rebelled," nor in districts where the "rebellion" had been suppressed. In sober fact, it applied to the slaves only in areas where the national government as yet had no authority. Yet it was nevertheless an immortal blow for human freedom. It not only changed the aims of the war, but it raised them to a higher level. Infusing a new moral meaning into the conflict, it deepened that element of passion and inspiration which vibrated in so many of Lincoln's utterances. It rallied the liberal thought of Britain and the globe to the Union side. Month by month, year by year, it had a widening influence. "Great," wrote Emerson, "is the virtue of this Proclamation. It works when men are sleeping, when the army goes into winter quarters, when generals are treacherous or imbecile." In its way, it is working still.

Yet the idea that the Southern people had rights in the matter which should be respected was one which Lincoln never lost. When he talked with Alexander H. Stephens at the Hampton Roads conference in 1865, he took care to explain his course and expound his future hopes. Thus, writes Stephens:

He said it was not his intention in the beginning to interfere with slavery in the States; that he never would have done it, if he had not been compelled by necessity to do it, to maintain the Union; that the subject presented many difficult and perplexing questions to him, that he had hesitated for some time, and had resorted to this measure, only when driven to it by public necessity; that he had been in favor of the General Government prohibiting the extension of slavery into the Territories, but did not think that that Government possessed power over the subject in the States, except as a war measure; and that he had always himself been in favor of emancipation, but not immediate emancipation, even by the States.

He went on to say that he would be willing to be taxed to remunerate the Southern people for their slaves. He believed that the people of the North were as responsible for slavery as the people of the South, and if the war should then cease, with the voluntary abolition of slavery by the States, he should be in favor, individually, of the Government paying a fair indemnity for the loss to the owners. He said he believed this feeling had an extensive existence at the North. He knew some who would be in favor of an appropriation as high as four hundred millions of dollars for this purpose.

3

This passage, so clearly stamped by kindliness toward the Southern people, brings us to another consideration. As it was Jefferson Davis's special task to create a nation, it was Lincoln's to maintain a nation; to consolidate Northern sentiment, to lift the Northern heart, and to keep an effective Northern majority behind him. He did it by sagacious measures, and by a constant appeal to idealism and moral passion of the people. But it was not merely the internal harmony of the North of which he thought; he equally kept in mind the future harmony of the whole nation. He looked forward to a restoration not merely of the physical Union, but of the old Union of hearts and affections. The nation could not long be pinned together by bayonets; it would have to be pinned together by the common memories, common culture and ideas, and common aims in building the future, which had been the cement of Union in the past. Throughout the conflict he never indulged in any word that would heighten the tides of anger, vengefulness, and malice that swept the land. On the contrary, he always tried to repress sectional animosities, reduce the hatreds of war, and mollify the nation's temper. Jefferson Davis several times heaped bitter imprecations upon the North; but Lincoln never once spoke unkindly of the Southern people, and never went beyond a measured severity even in condemning those he considered their worst demagogues. As James G. Randall puts it:

In earliest life, in years of growth, in love and friendship, in the family circle, in the tough substance of democratic thought, Lincoln's mind and character were moulded by Southern influences. In wistfulness for other days when sectionalism was raging, in the midst of tragic strife as at Gettysburg, where he uttered not a syllable of hatred, Lincoln gave evidence of Southern understanding. In his closeness to border State opinion, in his design for freedom, in incidents of presidential helpfulness to friends on the other side, and at the last in his pattern for peace without vindictiveness, Lincoln kept his sympathy for the people of the South.

This course was an essential part of his statesmanship. He had to preserve a nation; and the only nation worth preserving was one of brotherly kinship and affection.

Campbell-Bannerman during the South African War was profoundly aware that the Boers would have to be lived with after the conflict; he indulged in no unkind word or gesture; the Afrikanders, he said, "must be taken to our bosom." He was but following Lincoln's example.

The golden thread of concern for national unity can be traced through the whole administration. In December, 1861, Lincoln told Congress that three vacancies existed in the Supreme Court. "I have so far forborne from making nominations to fill these vacancies," he added, "for reasons which I will now state. Two of the outgoing judges resided within the States now overrun by revolt; so that if successors were appointed in the same localities, they could not now serve upon their circuits; and many of the most competent men there probably would not take the personal hazard of accepting to serve, even here, upon the Supreme Bench. I have been unwilling to throw all the appointments northward, thus disabling myself from doing justice to the South on the return of peace; although I may remark that to transfer to the North one which has heretofore been in the South would not, with reference to territory and population, be unjust."

We can guess how happy Lincoln would have been could he have known that before many decades elapsed a Louisianian would be Chief Justice. In 1863, just after Gettysburg, General Meade issued some general orders which both pained and irritated Lincoln; for in these orders Meade spoke of "driving the invaders from our soil." To Lincoln every foot of the nation's land was "our soil"— and this unhappy phrase rankled in his mind as he wrote a stern letter of rebuke to Meade. We all know how mild and generous was Lincoln's plan of reconstruction, and how mildly and generously he had it applied, first in Louisiana, then in Arkansas, and lastly in Tennessee. We all know how decisively he intervened on behalf of the South when Congress in the Wade-Davis bill of 1864 arrogated to itself (quite unconstitutionally, as Lincoln believed) the power to destroy slavery within the States, and prescribed a much harsher scheme of reconstruction. His secretaries preserve the constitutional lesson he administered to Zack Chandler:

> Chandler: "The important point [in the bill] is that one prohibiting slavery in the reconstructed States."
> Lincoln: "This is the very point on which I doubt the authority of Congress to act."
> Chandler: "It is no more than you have done yourself!"
> Lincoln: "I conceive that I may in an emergency do things on military grounds which cannot be done constitutionally by Congress."

Few scenes in our Presidential history are so remarkable as that of the first Cabinet meeting after the Hampton Roads Conference, at which Lincoln had talked of peace with Alexander H. Stephens and R. M. T. Hunter. The date was February 5, 1865; Southern defeat was now certain; it was clear that the spring offensive would bring the fall of Richmond. Lee's surrender was in fact but two months away. Yet to that night meeting of the Cabinet Lincoln submitted a plan for paying $400,000,000 to the Southern States, in proportion to their slave populations, in return for an early termination of hostilities; all political offenses to be pardoned, and all property except slaves to be released from confiscation or forfeiture. It is clear that he had a larger object in view than the shortening of the war by a few weeks. He wished to bring the Southern States back on terms that fell short of total subjugation; to give the impoverished Southern people a fund with which to begin rebuilding their economy; and by an act of sweeping generosity to lay the foundation for a Union of hearts, not of force. His regret when the Cabinet unanimously disapproved of his plan was strongly expressed, and for a time he hoped to revive it. One of his last acts on the day of his assassination was to hold a conference with James W. Singleton, once of Virginia and later of Quincy, Illinois, on plans for reconstructing Virginia under the Pierpont Government.

It was with good reason that the Richmond *Whig* began its editorial of Monday, April 17, on the assassination of Lincoln, with the words: "The heaviest blow which has ever fallen upon the people of the South has descended."

All this is proof of Lincoln's statesmanship—but he was something more than a statesman. Herbert Croly included in his book, *The Promise of American Life,* a chapter entitled "Lincoln As More Than an American"—one of the best short estimates of Lincoln's career ever written. His thesis was that while Lincoln is often called a typical American, in actuality he was very untypical. In an era and region where most men looked down upon education—at any rate, any high degree of education—he carefully trained and filled his mind; using for this purpose precisely the right instruments—Euclid, who taught him exactness; the Bible, which taught him moral elevation; and Shakespeare, who taught him humanity. In an environment where men were careless and undisciplined, Lincoln trained himself to be highly self-controlled, patient, and watchful. At a time when the country admired reckless, aggressive, self-willed men like Jackson, Lincoln was magnanimous, thoughtful, considerate of every interest, and restrained. Croly's appraisal was just—Lincoln was a good deal more than a typical American. For somewhat different reasons, we may say that he was more than a statesman—more than a Bismarck or Cavour.

4

A supreme realist, in one respect he was often ready to abandon realism. That is, he was ready, on fit occasion, to appeal to a spirit of idealism and generosity which hardly existed—which was almost imperceptible—but which his appeal could sometimes call into being; a coal of finer feeling which his example and his simple eloquence could sometimes fan into flame. We have said that he almost always addressed himself to men who differed from him, not to friends, and that he appealed to their reason, not their prejudices and emotions. He did more than this: he appealed to their better selves. And his appeal to the country at large was an appeal to its nobler side, its better nature.

In three positive respects he tried to awaken the idealism and enlarge the vision of the people. To begin with, he never ceased to tell the Northerners, at least after the summer of 1862, that the struggle they were maintaining was essentially a moral struggle. He thought it a plain moral axiom that the black man should have the same right as the white man to eat the bread he had earned by the sweat of his brow. He wanted all men everywhere to be free. He knew that the North was as responsible for slavery as the South; he tolerated it as a parent would tolerate a snake found in bed with the children—it must be killed in a way that would not inflict needless injury on those burdened with it; but he always thought the institution, as an institution, immoral.

In the second instance, Lincoln never ceased to insist that the war was a struggle for the vindication of democracy in the sight of all mankind; a war for the renovation of democratic government, so that its example could be kept effective to all other people. When at Gettysburg he interpreted the meaning of the conflict, it was in these terms of the necessity of preserving the great American example for the struggling and oppressed of other lands. The dead had given the last full measure of devotion not merely for the Union, and not merely for the ending of slavery, but that the nation should have a rebirth of freedom, and that popular government should lift a brighter torch than ever. The survival of that government with undimmed lustre actually was of the first importance to struggling democracy in Great Britain, in France, and in other lands. If, in the Grant Administration, the torch burned with a murky stench, it was still there, and men knew that the flame could be purified, as in no great time it was.

And, in the third instance, Lincoln more than once touched upon a yet larger concept. He had a vision of the immense and he hoped gradually brightening future of mankind. Indeed, he alone among nineteenth century statesmen after the generation of Madison and Jefferson seems to have had that vision. He realized that the political and social life of mankind is only in its beginnings, that it will develop through long ages to come, and that we do not act for our generation or the next alone but for countless generations to follow. In his letter of May 19, 1862, he had appealed to the border States to adopt gradual emancipation in just these terms. They must do their duty with a sense that it would affect coming centuries, ran his argument. "May the vast future not have to lament that you have neglected it."

He saw that the American conflict, so terrible an agony to those caught in its coils, would yet appear but as one brief event in the long march of mankind to happier goals. His fullest expression of his concept appeared in his noble letter of August 26, 1863, to J. C. Conkling of Springfield; a letter written when the nation had emerged from the terrible anxieties of Gettysburg and Vicksburg to find that its path ahead seemed clearer. "The signs look better," wrote Lincoln, in phrasing worthy of Shakespeare:

The Father of Waters again goes unvexed to the sea. Thanks to the great Northwest for it; nor yet wholly to them. Three hundred miles up they met New England, Empire, Keystone, and Jersey, hewing their way right and left. The sunny South, too, in more colors than one, lent a helping hand. On the spot their part of the history was jotted down in black and white. The job was a great national one, and let none be slighted who bore an honorable part in it. And while those who have cleared the great river may well be proud, even that is not all. It is hard to say that anything has been more bravely or well done than at Antietam, Murfreesboro, Gettysburg, and on many fields of less note. Nor must Uncle Sam's web feet be forgotten. At all the watery margins they have been present, not only on the deep sea, the broad bay, and the rapid river, but also up the narrow muddy bayou, and wherever the ground was a little damp, they have been and made their tracks.

And then came the climactic sentence, one of the noblest Lincoln ever wrote:

Thanks to all. For the great Republic,—for the principle it lives by and keeps alive,—for man's vast future,—thanks to all.

In this concept that the American Civil War was a struggle for the future of humanity, Lincoln joined hands with the Revolutionary statesmen—Washington, Jefferson, Madison, Adams—who had a vision of the creation of a new and brighter civilization; who believed that they were throwing open the gates to a higher, better future for all men. He became more than a statesman—he was a seer, a prophet, a poet. Recently, since 1950, American boys have died in the rice fields and on the mountains of Korea—for what? For the United States, for justice and democracy, but above all for a still larger cause—for the United Nations and for the orderly free progress of mankind.

We Americans shall doubtless meet great crises in the future, as we have met them in the past. In some of these crises, no doubt, superhuman exertions may well again be needed. To those who will have to bear the strain and agony, there will echo down the inspiring words of the great seer of the year 1863: "Thanks to all. For the great Republic,—for the principle it lives by and keeps alive,— *for man's vast future,*—thanks to all."

Chapter 7

Breakdown of Statesmanship: The Glorious and the Terrible Sides of War

EVERY GREAT WAR has two sides, the glorious and the terrible. The glorious is perpetuated in multitudinous pictures, poems, novels, statues: in Meissonier's canvases of Friedland and Austerlitz, Byron's stanzas on Waterloo and Tennyson's on the Light and Heavy brigades, St. Gaudens's Sherman riding forward victory-crowned, Freeman's "Lee." The terrible is given us in a much slighter body of memorabilia: Jacques Callot's gruesome etchings of the Thirty Years War, Goya's paintings of French atrocities in Spain, Zola's "The Debacle," Walt Whitman's hospital sketches, and the thousand-page novels that drearily emerged from the Second World War.

The two aspects do exist side by side. Every student of war comes upon hundreds of veracious descriptions of its pomp and pageantry, innumerable tales of devotion and heroism. They exalt the spirit. Yet every such student falls back from this exaltation upon a sombre remembrance of the butchery, the bereavement, and the long bequest of poverty, exhaustion, and despair. In observing the centenary of the Civil War, every sensible man should keep in mind that the conflict was a terrible reproach to American civilization and a source of poison and debilities still to be felt.

If it were not true that its debits far outweighed its credits, we might conclude that the republic would profit by a civil war in every generation, and that we should have commemorated Bull Run last July by again setting Yankee boys and Southern boys to killing each other. The mind recoils from the thought. But as the Civil War histories, novels, and motion pictures continue to pour forth, we shall be fortunate if we escape two very erroneous views.

The first view is that the war can somehow be detached from its context and studied as if it stood alone, without reference to causes or effects. War in fact, as Clausewitz long ago insisted, does not stand apart from and opposed to peace. It is simply a transfer of the normal inescapable conflicts of men from the realm of adjustment to that of violence. It represents not a complete transformation of national policy, but a continuance of policy by sanguinary means. That is, it cannot be understood without regarding both its causes and its results. Our Civil War, as Walt Whitman insisted, grew peculiarly out of national character. The other erroneous view is that the Civil War was, in the phrase of that graphic military historian Bruce Catton, a "Glory Road."

"Consider it not so deeply," Lady Macbeth says to her husband, stricken by the thought of red-handed murder; and "Consider it not so deeply," people instinctively say to those who remind them of war's inhuman massacre. Who wishes to while away an idle hour by looking at the harrowing pictures in the "Medical and Surgical History" of the war? It is a trick of human memories to forget, little by little, what is painful, and remember what is pleasant, and that tendency appertains to the folk memory as well. One of the finest descriptive pieces of the war was written by the true-hearted Theodore Winthrop, novelist and poet, just after his regiment crossed the Potomac on a spring night in 1861 to encamp on the Virginia side. It is rapturous in its depiction of the golden moon lighting a path over the river, the merry files of soldiers, the white tents being pitched in the dewy dawn. But ere long Winthrop was slain at Big Bethel in an engagement too blundering, shabby, and piteous for any pen. We remember the happy march but forget the death.

Or take two contrasting scenes later in the war, of the same day—the day of Malvern Hill, July 1, 1862. That battle of Lee and McClellan reached its climax in the gathering dusk of a lustrous summer evening, no breath of wind stirring the air. The Union army had placed its ranks and its artillery on the slope of a great hill, a natural amphitheatre, which the Southerners assaulted. Participants never forgot the magnificence of the spectacle. From the Confederate and Union guns stately columns of black smoke towered high in the blue sky. The crash of musketry and deeper thud of artillery; the thunder of gunboat mortars from the James River, their shells curving in fiery golden lines; the cavalry on either flank, galloping to attack; the foaming horses flying from point to point with aides carrying dispatches; the steady advance of the Confederate columns and the unyielding resistance of the dense Union lines; then as darkness gathered, the varicolored signal lights flashing back and forth their messages—all this made an unforgettable panorama.

But the sequel! The troops on both sides sank exhausted on their arms. From the field the shrieking and moaning of the wounded were heart-rending, yet nothing could be done to succor them. The sky grew overcast; intense darkness shut down; and at dawn came a fierce downpour. "Such rain, and such howling set up by the wounded," wrote one Southern soldier; "such ugly wounds, sickening to the sight even of the most hardened as the rain beat upon them, washing them to a pale purple; such long-fingered corpses, and in piles, too, like cordwood—may I never see the like again!"

Both novelist and poet almost instinctively turn to the heroic aspects and picturesque incidents of war. Lowell's "Commemoration Ode," one of the half-dozen finest pieces of literature born from the conflict, necessarily eulogizes the heroes; Mary Johnston's "The Long Roll," perhaps the best Southern war novel, celebrates the ardors, not the anguishes, of Stonewall Jackson's foot-cavalry; St. Gaudens's monument on Boston Common to Robert Gould Shaw and his black infantry—the men whose dauntless hearts beat a charge right up the red rampart's slippery swell—shows the fighters, not the fallen. The historian assists in falsifying the picture. Cold, objective, he assumes that both the glorious and horrible sides exist, and need no special emphasis. He thus tends to equate the two, although the pains and penalties of war far outweigh its gleams of grandeur.

Then, too, a problem of expression impedes the realistic writer. It is not difficult to describe the pageantry of Pickett's charge. But when we come to the costs, what can we say except that the casualties were 3,000 killed, 5,000 wounded? It is impossible to describe the agony of even one soldier dying of a gangrened wound, or the heartache of one mother losing her first born; what of 10,000 such soldiers and mothers? Moreover, most historians, like the novelists and poets, have an instinctive preference for the bright side of the coin. Henry Steele Commager's otherwise fine introduction to his valuable compilation "The Blue and The Gray" has much to say about gallantry and bravery, but nothing about the squalor, the stench, and the agony.

If we protest against the prettification of the Civil War, the thoughtless glorification of what was essentially a temporary breakdown of American civilization, we must do so with an acknowledgement that it did call forth many manifestations of an admirable spirit. The pomp and circumstance, the parade and pageantry, we may dismiss as essentially empty. The valor of the host of young men who streamed to the colors we may deeply admire, but as valor we may fortunately take it for granted, for most men are brave. The patriotic ardor displayed in the first months of the war may also be taken for granted. What was highly impressive was the serious, sustained conviction, the long-enduring dedication, of countless thousands on both sides for their chosen cause. This went far beyond the transient enthusiasms of Sumter and Bull Run; far beyond ordinary battlefield courage. Lecky was correct in writing: "That which invests war with a certain grandeur is the heroic self-sacrifice which it elicits." All life is in a real sense a conflict between good and evil, in which every man or woman plays a part. A host of young Americans felt that they were enlisted in this larger struggle, and regarded their service to the North or South as part of a lifetime service to the right.

Those who seek examples of this dedication can find them scattered throughout the war records. Lincoln specially admired his young friend Elmer Ellsworth, who had endured poverty and hardship with monastic devotion to train himself for service; Lee specially admired John Pelham, the daring artillerist. Both gave their lives. Some fine illustrations of the consecrated spirit can be found in the two volumes of the "Harvard Memorial Biographies" edited by Thomas Wentworth Higginson just after the war. The ninety-eight Harvard dead were no better than the farm lads from Iowa or Alabama, the clerks from New Orleans or New York, but some of them had special gifts of self-expression. Hearken, for example, to Colonel Peter A. Porter, who wrote in his last will and testament:

I can say, with truth, that I have entered on the course of danger with no ambitious aspirations, nor with the idea that I am fitted, by nature, or experience, to be of any important service to the government; but in obedi-

ence to the call of duty, demanding every citizen to con-
tribute what he could, in means, labor, or life, to sustain
the government of his country—a sacrifice made the
more willingly by me when I consider how singularly
benefitted I have been, by the institutions of the
land. . . .

As we distinguish between the shining glory of the war—
this readiness of countless thousands to die for an enduring
moral conviction—and the false or unimportant glories, so
we must distinguish between the major and the lesser debits
of the conflict. Some evils and mischiefs which seemed
tremendous at the time have grown less in the perspective
of years; some which at first appeared small now loom
large.

It was one of the bloodiest of all wars; the total deaths
in the Union and Confederate armies have been computed
at about 620,000; and one of the facts which appalls any
careful student is the enormous amount of suffering on the
field and in the hospitals. The evidence of this, while not
within the view of general readers, is incontrovertible.
Armies the world over in 1860 were *worse* provided with
medical and surgical facilities than in Napoleon's day. The
United States, after its long peace, began the war with
practically no medical service whatever. Surgical application of the ideas of Pasteur and Lister lay in the future.
Almost every abdominal wound meant death. Any severe
laceration of a limb entailed amputation, with a good
chance of mortal gangrene of erysipelas. The North syste-
matically prevented shipments of drugs and surgical instruments to the South, a measure which did not shorten
the conflict by a day, but cost the Southern troops untold
agony. Had it not been for the Sanitary Commission, a
body privately organized and supported, Northern armies
would have duplicated the experience of British forces in
the Crimea; yet Secretary of War Stanton at first deliberately impeded the Commission's work.

The story of battle after battle was the same. Night descended on a field ringing with cries of agony: Water! Water! Help!—if in winter, Blankets! Cover! All too frequently no help whatever was forthcoming. After some great conflicts the wounded lay for days, and sometimes a week, without rescue. Shiloh was fought on a Sunday and Monday. Rain set in on Sunday night, and the cold April drizzle continued through Tuesday night. On Tuesday morning nine-tenths of the wounded still lay where they fell; many had been there forty-eight hours without attention; numbers had died of shock or exhaustion; some had even drowned as the rain filled depressions from which they could not crawl. Every house in the area was converted into a hospital, where the floors were covered with wretches heavily wounded, sometimes with arms or legs torn off, who after the first bandage, got no nursing, medical care, or even nourishment. "The first day or two," wrote a newspaper reporter, "the air was filled with groans, sobs, and frenzied curses, but now the sufferers are quiet; not from cessation of pain, but mere exhaustion." Yet at this time the war was a year old.

Still more poignant versions of the same story might be given. Lee and Pope fought Second Manassas on the last Friday and Saturday in August, 1862, so near Washington that groups standing on housetops in the capital heard the rumble of artillery. The battleground, five miles long and three wide, was thickly strewn with dead and wounded. Pope retreated in confusion; many in Washington feared the city might be taken. In these circumstances, as late as the following Wednesday one member of the inadequate body of surgeons estimated that 2,000 wounded had received no attention. Many had not tasted food for four days; some were dying of hunger and thirst. A reporter for the Washington *Republican* wrote on Thursday that some dying men could yet be saved by prompt help. And on Friday, a week after the battle began, a correspondent of the New York *Tribune* told of heart-rending scenes as the doctors searched among heaps of putrefying dead men for men yet clinging to life—men who, when anyone approached, would cry, "Doctor, come to *me;* you look like a kind man; for God's sake come to *me.*"

Anyone who is tempted to think of Gettysburg only in terms of its heroic episodes, its color and drama, should turn to the pages in "Battles and Leaders" in which General John D. Imboden describes the transport of the Confederate wounded, after their defeat, back into Maryland. He was ordered to ride to the head of the long wagon column as, in darkness and storm, it moved south:

For four hours I hurried forward on my way to the front, and in all that time I was never out of hearing of the groans and cries of the wounded and dying. Scarcely one in a hundred had received adequate surgical aid, owing to the demands on the hard-working surgeons from still worse cases that had to be left behind. Many of the wounded in their wagons had been without food for thirty-six hours. Their torn and bloody clothing, matted and hardened, was rasping the tender, inflamed, and still oozing wounds. Very few of the wagons had even a layer of straw in them, and all were without springs. The road was rough and rocky from the heavy washings of the preceding day. The jolting was enough to have killed strong men, if long exposed to it. From nearly every wagon as the teams trotted on, urged by whip and shout, came such cries and shrieks as these:

"My God! Why can't I die?"

"My God! Will no one have mercy and kill me?"

"Stop! Oh, for God's sake stop just for one minute; take me out and leave me to die on the roadside."

Occasionally a wagon would be passed from which only low, deep moans could be heard. No help could be rendered to any of the sufferers. No heed could be given to any of their appeals. Mercy and duty to the many forbade the loss of a moment in the vain effort then and there to comply with the prayers of the few. On! On! We must move on. The storm continued and the darkness was appalling. There was no time even to fill a canteen with water for a dying man; for, except the drivers and the guards, all were wounded and utterly helpless in that vast procession of misery. During this one night I realized more of the horrors of war than I had in all the preceeding two years.

After such a description, we can understand why a radical Northern Senator, looking across the battlefield of the Wilderness as fighting ended, told Hugh McCulloch that if in 1861 he had been given one glimpse of the agonies he there beheld, he would have said to the South: "Erring sisters, go in peace." John Esten Cooke was right in his elegy for Pelham; the living were brave and noble, but the dead were the bravest of all.

Yet *this* was far from being the ugliest side of war. Nor was the suffering in the huge prison camps, South and North, part of the worst side of war; the suffering which MacKinlay Kantor describes in his novel and to which Benét briefly adverts in "John Brown's Body":

> *The triple stockade of Anderson-*
> *ville the damned.*
> *Where men corrupted like flies in*
> *their own dung*
> *And the gangrened sick were black*
> *with smoke and their filth.*

What maims the bodies of men is less significant than what maims their spirit.

One ugly aspect of the Civil War too generally ignored is the devastation, more and more systematic, that accompanied it. For three reasons too little has been said of this devastation; the facts were kept out of official reports, the tale is too painful, and the recital easily becomes monotonous. Yet by 1862 the war in the South had become one of general depredation; by 1863, of wanton destruction; and by 1864, of an organized devastation which in terms of property anticipated the worst chapters of the two world wars. Georgia and the Shenandoah suffered in 1864 almost precisely as Belgium and Serbia suffered in 1914—the executions omitted. It was barbaric, and the only excuse to be made is that war is barbarism.

The turning point in the attitude of Northern military men was reached when General John Pope on July 18, 1862, issued from Washington headquarters a set of Draconian general orders. Order No. 5 directed that the army should subsist as far as practicable upon the country, giving vouchers for supplies seized. Order No. 7 decreed the summary execution of persons caught firing upon Union troops from houses. Order No. 11 (five days later) required officers to arrest immediately all disloyal males within reach, to make them take the oath of allegiance or go South, and to shoot all who violated their oath or who returned from the Confederacy. The order for living on the country, widely publicized East and West, changed the attitude of troops, and inspired private looting as well as public seizures of property. Pope was soon ousted, but the moral effect of his orders persisted.

Though most of the facts were excluded from official reports, their sum total, insofar as one shrewd observer could arrive at it, may be found in John T. Trowbridge's graphic volume written in 1866, "A Picture of the Desolated States." In his preface Trowbridge speaks of the Union forces not as our heroic armies but our destroying armies. Even this practiced reporter is less graphic, however, than the people who suffered under the onslaught and wrote while their emotions, like their property, still burned. Hear a lady of Louisiana tell what occurred when N. P. Banks's army passed:

I was watching from my window the apparently orderly march of the first Yankees that appeared in view and passed up the road, when, suddenly, as if by magic, the whole plantation was covered with men, like bees from an overthrown hive; and, as far as my vision extended, an inextricable medley of men and animals met my eye. In one place, excited troopers were firing into the flock of sheep; in another, officers and men were in pursuit of the boys' ponies, and in another, a crowd were in excited chase of the work animals. The kitchen was soon filled with some, carrying off the cooking utensils and the provisions of the day; the yard with others, pursuing the poultry. . . . They penetrated under the house, into the outbuildings, and into the garden, stripping it in a moment of all its vegetables. . . . This continued during the day . . . and amid a bewildering sound of oaths and imprecations. . . . When the army had passed, we were left destitute.

Sherman believed in total war; that is, in waging war not only against the Southern armies, but the Southern people. His theory was that every man, woman, and child was "armed and at war." He wrote his wife in the summer of 1862 that the North might fall into bankruptcy, "but if they can hold on the war will soon assume a turn to extermination, not of soldiers alone, that is the least part of the trouble, but the people." He denied, in effect, that Southerners had a right to resist invasion. When Union steamers were fired on near Randolph, Mississippi, in the fall of 1862, he destroyed Randolph, and a little later had all houses, farms, and cornfields devastated for fifteen miles along the banks.

When he drove his red plowshare across Georgia and the Carolinas, his object was to leave only scorched earth behind. He had already written of his Western operations: "Not a man is to be seen; nothing but women with houses plundered, fields open to the cattle and horses, pickets lounging on every porch, and desolation sown broadcast; servants all gone, and women and children bred in luxury . . . begging . . . for soldiers' rations." His aim was that which Phil Sheridan avowed: to leave them nothing but their eyes to weep with.

The final devastation of half the South was horrible to behold, and it was distressing to think that these savage losses had been inflicted by Americans upon fellow Americans. Yet this was far from being the worst aspect of the conflict, or the least easily reparable. Damages on which we can fix the dollar sign are important not in themselves, but as they become translated into cultural and spiritual losses; into the intellectual retardation caused by poverty, for example. The physical recovery of the South was rapid. As it was primarily an agricultural section, a few good crops at fair prices did much to restore it; and the swiftness with which housing, railroads, bridges, and public facilities were rebuilt astonished observers of the 1870s just as the swift postwar recovery of Germany and Poland has astonished observers of our day.

Infinitely worse were the biological losses—the racial hurts—inflicted by the Civil War. The killing of between 600,000 and 700,000 young men in a nation of 33,000,000 and the maiming or permanent debilitation of as many more had evil consequences projected into the far-distant future. We lost not only these men, but their children, and their children's children. Here, indeed, was a loss that proved highly cumulative. During the First World War, Lord Dunsany wrote a slender volume called "Tales of War." One of his apologues showed the Kaiser, as the embodiment of German militarism, commanded by a spirit to come on a tour. They crossed the German plain to a neat garden. Look, said the spirit:

The Kaiser looked; and saw a window shining and a neat room in a cottage; there was nothing dreadful there, thank the good German God for that; it was all right, after all. The Kaiser had had a fright, but it was all right; there was only a woman with a baby sitting before a fire; and two small children and a m·n. And it was quite a jolly room. And the man was a young soldier; and, why, he was a Prussian Guardsman—there was a helmet hanging on the wall—so everything was all right. They were jolly German children; that was well. How nice and homely the room was. . . . The firelight flickered, and the lamp shone on, and the children played on the floor, and the man was smoking out of a china pipe; he was strong and able and young, one of the wealth-winners of Germany.

"Have you seen?" asked the phantom.

"Yes," said the Kaiser. . . .

At once the fire went out and the lamp faded away, the room fell sombrely into neglect and squalor, and the soldier and the children faded away with the room; all disappeared phantasmally, and nothing remained but the helmet in a kind of glow on the wall, and the woman sitting all by herself in the darkness.

"It has all gone," said the Kaiser.

"It has never been," said the phantom.

The Kaiser looked again. Yes, there was nothing there, it was just a vision. . . .

"It might have been," said the phantom.

Just so, we can say that the multitude of Civil War dead represent hundreds of thousands of homes, and hundreds of thousands of families, that might have been, and never were. They represent millions of people who might have been part of our population today and are not. We have lost the books they might have written, the scientific discoveries they might have made, the inventions they might have perfected. Such a loss defies measurement.

The only noteworthy attempt to measure the biological losses was made by David Starr Jordan and his son Harvey in a volume called "War's Aftermath" (1914). The authors circulated carefully drawn questionnaires in Spottsylvania and Rockbridge Counties in Virginia, and in Cobb County in Georgia, inquiring particularly into the eugenic effects of the conflict. One of their queries brought out evidence that by no means all casualties were among the men; numerous girls and women succumbed to the hardships and anxieties of the conflict in the South. Another question elicited unanimous agreement that "the flower of the people" went into the war at the beginning, and of these a large part died before the end. President Jordan, weighing all the responses, reached two conclusions: first, that the evidence "leaves a decided evidence in favor of grave racial hurt," and second, that "the war has seriously impoverished this country of its best human values."

Even the terrible loss of young, productive lives, the grave biological injury to the nation, however, did not constitute the worst side of the war. One aspect of the conflict was still more serious. It was the aspect to which Lowell referred in lines written a few years after Appomattox:

> *I looked to see an ampler atmosphere*
> *By that electric passion-gust blown clear*
> *I looked for this; consider what I hear. . . .*
>
> *Murmur of many voices in the air*
> *Denounces us degenerate,*
> *Unfaithful guardians of a noble fate. . . .*

The war, as Walt Whitman truly said, had grown out of defects in the American character; of American faults it cured few, accentuated a number, and gave some a violently dangerous trend. Far behind the lines, it added to the already discreditable total of violence in American life. Applying to industry a great forcing-draft, the bellows of huge wartime appropriations, it strengthened the materialistic forces in our civilization. Its state and federal contracts, its bounty system, its innumerable opportunities for battening on the nation's woes, made speculation fashionable, and corruption almost too common for comment. Its inflation bred extravagance and dissipation.

Every month heightened the intolerance of war; it began with mobs in New York threatening newspaper offices, a mob in Philadelphia trying to lynch Senator James A. Bayard, and mobs in the South flogging and exiling Union men; as it went on, freedom of speech almost disappeared over broad areas. The atmosphere of war fostered immorality; Richmond and Washington alike became filled with saloons, brothels, and gambling dens, and such occupied cities as Memphis and Nashville were sinks of iniquity. For every knightly martyr like James Wadsworth or Albert Sidney Johnston there arose two such coarse, aggressive, selfish careerists as Ben Butler and Dan Sickles. Wadsworth and Johnston died in battle, but Butler and Sickles remained to follow postwar political careers. Seen in perspective, the war was a gigantic engine for coarsening and lowering the American character even while it quickened certain of our energies.

Parson Brownlow, a Tennessee Unionist, went from city to city in the North in 1862 demanding "grape for the Rebel masses, and hemp for their leaders"; saying that he himself would tie the rope about the necks of some rebel generals; calling for the confiscation of all Southern property; proclaiming that he would be glad to arm every wolf, bear, catamount, and crocodile, every devil in hell, to defeat the South; and declaring he would put down the rebellion "if it exterminates from God's green earth every man, woman, and child south of Mason and Dixon's Line."

In the South two famous leaders, Robert Toombs and Howell Cobb, united that year in an address to their people just as vitriolic. "The foot of the oppressor is on the soil of Georgia," it began. "He comes with lust in his eye, poverty in his purse, and hell in his heart. How shall you meet him? . . . With death for him or for yourself!" Better the charnel house for every Southerner, they continued, than "loathsome vassalage to a nation already sunk below the contempt of the civilized world." Thaddeus Stevens nursed his hatred until he spoke of "exterminating" or driving into exile *all* Southerners, just as Sherman declared he would "slay millions" to assure the safety of the Mississippi. Women of the South meanwhile expressed the most vindictive detestation of all Yankees. "I hate them," wrote one Mississippi woman after a raid on her community, "more now than I did the evening I saw them sneaking off with all we cared for, and so it will be every day I live."

Hatred was seen in its most naked form in those communities divided against themselves and racked by guerrilla war; in Missouri, Arkansas, parts of Kentucky, and East Tennessee. Writes Charles D. Drake, a distinguished Missouri leader, of his state: "Falsehood, treachery, and perjury pervaded the whole social fabric." He went on: "Could there be written a full account of all the crimes of the rebels of Missouri, and the outrages and wrongs inflicted by them upon her loyal inhabitants, during the four years of the rebellion, the world would shrink aghast from a picture which has no parallel in the previous history of any portion of the Anglo-Saxon race." Confederate sympathizers in Missouri would have said the same of Union irregulars. One atrocity provoked another. These hatreds long survived the conflict, and indeed in some spots the embers still smoulder. Typifying the whole range of spiritual injuries wrought by the war, they justify the poet Blake's cry:

> *The soldier, armed with sword and gun,*
> *Palsied strikes the summer sun.*

The historian Mendelssohn Bartholdy, in his volume entitled "War and German Society," written as part of the Carnegie Endowment's huge economic history of World War I, concluded that the moral effects of war are much worse than the material effects. He also concluded that they are radically bad, for they strike at the very heart of a country's character; "modern war, with its robot-like disregard of individual values, is bound to make the peculiar virtue of a nation an object of attack." As respects the Civil War, we can agree. If it was necessary for preserving the Union and extinguishing slavery, it was of course worth more than it cost; but should it have been necessary? Could not better leadership from 1830 to 1860 have averted it? This is a bootless question. But it is certain that the conflict, so much the greatest convulsion in our history, so tremendous in its impact on our national life, so fascinating in its drama, was in spite of all compensating elements, all the heroism, all the high example we find in Lee's character and Lincoln's wisdom, materially a disaster and morally a tragedy.

It is unfortunate that of the flood of books on the war ninety-nine in a hundred are on military topics and leaders, and that a great majority fasten attention on the floating banners, the high-ringing cheers, the humors of the camp, the ardors of the charge; the whole undeniable fascination and romance of the first true *volkskrieg* in history. It is right, within measure, to let them lift our hearts. But the long commemoration will pass essentially unimproved if it does not give us a deeper, sterner, more scientific study of the collision of two creeds and two ways of life as related to an examination of war in general.

We should probe more deeply into its roots, a process that will expose some of the weaknesses of our social fabric and governmental system. We should pay fuller attention to its darker aspects, and examine more honestly such misrepresentations as the statement it was distinguished by its generosity of spirit, the magnanimity with which the combatants treated each other; a statement absurd on its face, for no war which lasts four years and costs 600,000 lives leaves much magnanimity in its later phases. We should above all examine more closely the effects of the great and terrible war not on the nation's politics—we know that; not on its economy—we also know that; but on its character, the vital element of national life.

This examination will lead into unpleasant paths, and bring us to unhappy conclusions; but it will profit us far more than stirring battle canvasses. All nations must be schooled in such studies if the world is ever to find an answer to a question uttered just after World War I by William E. Borah, a question that still rings in men's ears: "When shall we escape from war? When shall we loosen the grip of the monster?"